INSIGHT COM

Ice[...]

C000163551

Compact Guide: Iceland is the ultimate quick-reference guide to this fascinating destination. It tells you all you need to know about Iceland's attractions, from its glaciers and geothermal springs to its waterfalls and volcanoes, not forgetting its picturesque settlements and its lively capital, Reykjavík.

This is one of 130 Compact Guides, combining the interests and enthusiasms of two of the world's best-known information providers: Insight Guides, whose innovative titles have set the standard for visual travel guides since 1970, and Discovery Channel, the world's premier source of nonfiction television programming.

Discovery CHANNEL

APA PUBLICATIONS L
Part of the Langenscheidt Publishing Group

Star Attractions

An instant reference to some of Iceland's most popular tourist attractions to help you set your priorities.

Hallgrímskirkja p20

The Blue Lagoon p25

Lake Mývatn p35

Jökulsárgljúfur National Park p39

Skálafellsjökull p45

Þórsmörk Valley p49

Skógafoss p49

Snæfellsjökull p54

Látrabjarg p59

Gullfoss p65

Hveravellir p68

Iceland

Introduction

Iceland – A Young Country 5
Historical Highlights 14

Places

Route 1: Reykjavík 18
Route 2: Along the Ring Road through Iceland's
west and north 28
Route 3: Along the Ring Road through Iceland's
east and south 42
Route 4: Circular tour via Snæfellsnes and through
the Westfjords 53
Route 5: Iceland for beginners and short-stay visitors 63
Route 6: Crossing the central highlands 67
Route 7: From the bathing lake in hell to the steaming glacier ... 70

Culture

Literature and Music 73
Events Calendar 75

Leisure

Food and Drink 77
Active Holidays 81

Practical Information

Getting There 83
Getting Around 84
Facts for the Visitor 90
Accommodation 95

Index 104

Iceland – A Young Country

A medieval manuscript tells the tale of Flóki Vilgerðarson, who in 864 attempted to settle on this remote island in the North Sea. Flóki's endeavours were thwarted because when he landed in spring and encountered idyllic conditions, he gave little thought to storing up provisions for the coming winter. When the cold months arrived, the cattle that he had brought with him perished through lack of feed. Before leaving the island he gave it the name of Iceland. Ironically, when Iceland's much icier neighbour to the west was discovered 100 years later, it was given the name of Greenland.

A good tenth of Iceland's surface area does justice to its name. Some 11,800 sq. km (4,556 sq. miles) is covered by glacial ice. But that is not the whole country by a long way. Other landscape features include volcanoes and fjords, meadows and barren wastes, hot springs and deafening waterfalls – Iceland is a country of great diversity. At first sight it seems raw, primeval and in some way incomplete, but on closer inspection it reveals a quiet and attractive face. Unexpected colours and shapes can be found in newly formed lava, beside small streams or by hot pots, the thermal springs where mineral deposits have been shaped by nature into works of art. Iceland's flora also paints bright colours on to the island's canvas. Meadows, swathed with cotton grass like white clouds, are covered in violet carpets of Arctic fireweed amid the wastes of the otherwise barren uplands: when in flower a vivid, pioneer plant standing out against a background of scree that extends as far as the horizon.

The snow-capped Snæfellsjökull

5

Iceland cannot boast any famous historic monuments, world-ranking museums or grand castles, but that doesn't mean that the island has nothing cultural to offer. The museums that do document Icelandic art, history and people are well run and certainly worth a visit, if newcomers to the island are to find out more about this fascinating country and its inhabitants.

Gentian

Human existence on the island of Iceland only points the way; it never has any impact on the scenery. Even Reykjavík, the island's undisputed capital, is characterised much more by the surrounding mountains than by the pervasive concrete architecture.

At home in eastern Iceland

Background and geology

Geologically, Iceland is one of the world's youngest nations. According to the theory that explains the development of the continents, back in the very early days of the earth's history, one large continental mass broke up into several continental plates and over a period lasting millions of years these plates drifted apart. The American

and Eurasian (Europe and Asia) continents were once joined together and the mid-Atlantic ridge, upon which Iceland lies, is the seam between the two plates. It is visible in a number of places on the island, in the Þingvellir National Park *(see page 66)*, for example. The famous Almannagjá rift has, over the past 20 years, widened by 10cm (4 ins). It is thus possible to say that the east of Iceland belongs on the European side, the west of Iceland to the American side, and the middle is genuinely new land.

Lava sample

However, as the island occupies such a key position in geological terms, there is the risk that eruptions of molten lava could take place at any time. Since the island was first settled in the 9th century, there have been at least 150 eruptions, some of which lasted for years. The Westman Islands (Vestmannaejyar in Icelandic) off the south coast *(see page 50)* have been created exclusively by volcanic action.

The latest major eruption to take place here was in 1973, when totally without warning a new volcano erupted on the eastern side of Heimaey town on the main island. In 1963, to the south of the Westman Islands and to the accompaniment of columns of fire, clouds of ash and rumbles of thunder, a completely new island emerged from the sea. It was called Surtsey after Surtr, the fire giant from Nordic mythology. The eruption lasted for three and a half years. By that time Surtsey had expanded to 2.5 sq. km (just under 1 sq. mile). Only scientists, keen to discover how new and isolated land is colonised by nature have access to it.

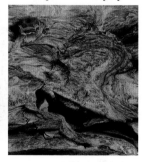

Eruptions can last for years

Geography

Iceland is an island republic in the North Atlantic. Its nearest neighbours are Greenland (287km/178 miles), the Faroe Islands (420km/261 miles), Scotland (798km/496 miles) and Norway (970km/603 miles). Given those distances, Iceland is clearly part of Europe.

The country covers an area of 103,000 sq. km (39,768 sq. miles), but only 20 percent of this area is available for use (including grassland). The rest is barren waste (54 percent), glacier (12 percent), lava (11 percent) or inland waters (3 percent). The longest river in Iceland is the Þjórsá (230km/143 miles); the largest natural lake, Þingvallavatn (83 sq km/32 sq miles); the largest inland lake, Þórisvatn (which serves as a reservoir for the hydro-electric power station on the Þjórsá); the highest waterfall, Glymur (190m/623ft; at the end of Hvalfjörpur); the highest mountain, Hvannadalschnúkur (2,119m/6,952ft); the largest ice-cap, Vatnajökull (8,400 sq. km/3,242 sq. miles); the largest island, Heimaey (13.4 sq. km/5.17 sq. miles).

Population

With only 2.5 people per sq. km, the total population of Iceland is about 275,000 – roughly the same as a smaller British city such as Plymouth – which makes it the most sparsely populated country in Europe. Less than two percent of the population are not native Icelanders (the largest group of immigrants is Scandinavian). At 83 for women, and 80 for men, life expectancy is well above the European average.

Around 60 percent of the population live in the metropolitan area of Reykjavík. Five of the 10 largest towns in the country are part of this conurbation. They are: Reykjavík (pop. 108,000), Kópavogur (pop. 20,000), Hafnarfjördur (pop. 18,500), Gardabær (pop. 7,800) and Mossfellsbœr (pop. 5,000).

The largest towns outside this region are Akureyri (just under 15,000), Reykjanesbær (Keflavík and neighbouring towns; pop. 10,400), Akranes (pop. 5,100), Heimaey (Westman Islands; pop. 4,600).

Climate and when to go

Iceland lies just south of the Arctic Circle, but the warm air from the Gulf Stream contributes to relatively settled weather patterns and for these latitudes mild temperatures. Winters are often severe with lots of rainfall, but an examination of the statistics reveals that Icelandic winters are no colder than those in much of northern continental Europe. Summers are cool with average temperatures in the region of 10°C (50°F).

Daytime temperatures of over 20°C (68°F) can be enjoyed in sheltered spots inland, more rarely in the coastal regions. In the central highlands night frosts are likely to occur throughout the year, in other parts of the country between the months of September and May.

Rainfall is highest on the southern slopes of the glaciers.

Peace and solitude

7

School photograph

Come well prepared

A country for all seasons

Icelandic sunset

The regions north of Vatnajökull generally have less rainfall. A characteristic feature of the island is rapid weather and wind changes. Visitors to Iceland are often reminded of the saying: 'If you don't like the weather, then just wait five minutes.'

The best time to visit Iceland is during the summer months of July and August. Evenings stay light from the middle of May to the end of August. At other times of the year the chances of seeing the Northern Lights are reasonably good as long as the nights are clear of cloud. Iceland does not experience polar nights, i.e. days without sunlight. The months of February, March and April are best for winter tours.

The midnight sun

Because the earth is tilted, the polar regions constantly face the sun at their respective summer solstices and face away from it in the winter. The Arctic and Antarctic circles at 66.5° north and south latitude respectively are the southern and northern limits of constant daylight on the longest day of the year.

While the offshore island of Grímsey straddles the Arctic Circle, the rest of Iceland lies to the south of the line. Akureyri is about 100km (60 miles) away. Although the sun does partially set on the summer solstice, Iceland's northern town enjoys very light evenings and it likes to describe itself as the 'town of the midnight sun'.

Iceland lies well to the west of the European mainland, but it stays in touch with European business time by using Greenwich Mean Time, even though the clocks should, according to the International Time Zone, be at least one hour, in western Iceland two hours, behind. Consequently, on the night of 21–22 June, the sun sets relatively late – after 1am – and then only for about 20 minutes.

Flora and fauna

Iceland's range of flora is influenced greatly by the country's position just south of the Arctic Circle. Grassland dominates on the extensive meadows, moorland and heaths. About 500 types of more advanced plants have been recorded, but mosses and lichens also abound. Because of Iceland's isolated position, little plant immigration has taken place. The harsh climate and also human influences, such as deforestation in the Middle Ages and overgrazing, mainly as a result of sheep farming, have restricted the spread of plant life.

Hardy vegetation

Apart from insects and fish, Icelandic fauna means almost exclusively birds. There are some 80 different species of breeding birds, including 16 types of ducks in Mýatn alone. About three dozen-plus species of migratory birds have been recorded as regular visitors to the island. Another 200 species have been sighted at least once. Maritime and wading birds make up the largest groups. The polar fox is the only native mammal; others, such as the mink, rat and reindeer, have been brought here by human beings.

Puffins breed in large numbers

The people

The Icelandic people are pragmatists. Their way of life may appear chaotic at times, but in fact they have a remarkable talent for organisation – many a tourist can tell a tale about that. They will not impose themselves upon their guests. It is not in their nature to be too familiar with strangers. In fact, they may come over as rather uncommunicative, but this does not mean that outsiders are rejected. It is more a sign of their cautious nature, more evident in the country than in the town. Another characteristic is the habit of not saying directly what they want, but to use circumlocutions to indicate what they don't want – but then that is just being sensitive to others.

There are, of course, differences between the 283,000-plus inhabitants. The young people who live in the capital, for example, grow up with very open-minded attitudes. As well as speaking Icelandic, nearly everyone speaks perfect English. Fashion trends from both sides of the Atlantic are quickly adopted. International culture, kept at bay for centuries because of Iceland's isolation, is now rapidly absorbed through satellite dishes, videos and CDs.

Feeding time in Reykjavík

Outdated and formal moral codes are alien to Icelanders. A third of all children are born outside marriage, but two-thirds of such children live in stable partnerships, generally equal in status to that of a legal marriage. About every 10th child grows up in a single-parent family.

Family names are used only in exceptional cases. The general rule is that a new addition to the family is given a first name and a surname, comprising the first name of

Church in Hafnarfjörđur

Farming and fishing

the father – seldom that of the mother – and the ending 'son' for son or 'dóttir' for daughter. Ásdís Magnúsdóttir and Guđmundur Gíslason, together with daughter Björk Guđmundsdóttir and son Grettir Guđmundsson, would constitute a typical Icelandic family. The surname is not usually used as a form of address. No one would say 'Hello, Ólafur Ragnar, son of Grimar', even if the person in question is the country's president. 'Hello, Ólafur', or in certain circumstances 'Hello, President Ólafur', would be the correct form of address.

Religion

More than 90 percent of the population belong to the Protestant Lutheran church. Roman Catholics, believers in ancient Germanic gods and other religious sects count for less than one percent each.

Language

Icelanders born in the 20th century are still able to read the literature of forebears born in the 12th and 13th centuries in the original language. This is because, unlike other European languages, their mother tongue has changed little since the Middle Ages. Even today it is regarded as important to keep the Icelandic language free of foreign influences. The English neologisms that have entered so many other languages have no place in Icelandic. Where necessary, new words are created. A fax, for example, is simply a '*símbréf*', or a 'telephone letter'. The word '*sími*' for telephone is derived from an old word meaning 'wire'.

Outsiders find it very difficult to get to grips with the Icelandic language because of some very complicated grammatical rules and unusual pronunciation. The only thing that is easy to grasp is the rule about emphasis. It is always the first syllable which is stressed. The many accents have nothing to do with emphasis. The everyday language for tourists is always English.

Economy

Fish has been the main impetus in the development of Iceland's economy. Two-thirds of the country's exports are fish products. For years, there have been problems arising from the overfishing of the waters around Iceland. Strict quotas will, it is hoped, lead to an improvement in fish stocks, but these restrictions have been responsible for many job losses. The unemployment rate, for decades an insignificant figure, rose to an unprecedented 5 percent in the middle of the 1990s.

Tourism has recently become the second most important sector in Iceland's economy, at least as far as foreign currency receipts are concerned. In one recent year, the island welcomed more than 230,000 visitors from all over the world, with Americans the largest group.

The heavily subsidised agricultural sector mainly supplies the domestic market. As a consequence of the drive to reduce soil erosion after freely grazing sheep reduced the sparse vegetation, flocks have been cut from almost 800,000 at the end of the 1980s to roughly half that figure. At the same time the number of horses has increased (today about 75,000).

Industrial development on an island that has few raw materials has been modest. But, given the cheap sources of power on the island, Iceland has become a desirable location for energy-intensive manufacturing processes, such as aluminium smelting. Other major exports are equipment for the fishing industry and software for various industries.

Horses and reindeer

Whaling

In 1985 Iceland ended commercial whaling, but allowed 'scientific' whaling to continue until 1989. At the time the country was open to criticism from Greenpeace. Iceland was also pilloried at international level, but no one tried to change the attitude of the Icelanders themselves by lending support to opponents of whaling there.

There is a long tradition of protecting whales in Iceland. As early as 1915 whaling was banned in Icelandic waters and this ruling lasted for 10 years. Iceland has never been one of the great whaling nations. In economic terms, the hunting of these giants of the sea has always been of little value. On the other hand, international calls for a boycott of Icelandic products had catastrophic consequences for the countries' fish exports.

Iceland's insistence on its right to continue whaling has to be seen as the protest of a small nation fed up with being bullied by the superpowers. Greenpeace and its militant wing, Sea Shepherd, viewed in Iceland, Greenland and the

Reykjavík harbour

There she blows!

Whale-watching at sunrise

A flag at the site of Iceland's first parliament at Þingvellir

Faroe Islands as a collection of idealists brought up in industrialised nations and alienated from nature, were painted as enemies of the state, even by Icelandic opponents of whaling.

In 1992 Iceland left the International Whaling Commission and, together with other North Atlantic nations, founded NAMMCO (North Atlantic Marine Mammal Commission). This body aims to preserve the whale, but also to allow whaling as long as it can be proved scientifically that whale stocks are not threatened.

In March 1999 the Icelandic parliament created the legal framework for whaling to begin again, but the government must give final approval. Whether it comes to that is in the end a finely balanced commercial decision. Whale-watching is now a rapidly-growing and lucrative tourist sideline. Tours are organised from Húsavík *(see page 38)*, Hvalfjörður *(see page 28)*, Ísafjörður *(see page 61)* and the harbours on the Suðurnes and Snæfellsnes *(see page 53)* peninsulas.

Politics

Under the constitution, the Icelandic parliament, the Althing, must be re-elected every four years, but circumstances often force elections to be brought forward. Protest parties are represented in the Althing and for many years, a non-dogmatic, environmentally orientated Women's Alliance was an important part of the political scene. Coalition governments are the rule rather than the exception.

Standing above the political fray is a directly elected president. Between 1980 and 1996, this office was held by the non-political Vigdís Finnbogadóttir. Her successor, the socialist and professional politician, Ólafur Ragnar Grímsson, would have had no chance against the popular ex-theatre director, had she decided to seek a fifth term.

Iceland is well represented in international organisations. It is a member of NATO but has no military forces of its own. But membership of economic groupings has always been a problem. Iceland became a member of EFTA in 1970 but this organisation no longer has any real significance in modern Europe. Until a few years ago entry into the European Union (EU) would have been inconceivable, given the fisheries policies adopted in Brussels. The political parties now adopt differing views on the issue. Iceland is currently part of the European Economic Area, an extension of the European Union, and enjoys the same status as Norway.

For historical reasons, Iceland has always maintained close links with the countries of northern Europe and is a member of the Nordic Council. Iceland, Greenland and the Faroe Islands make up the 'Vest Norden' region within which there are special economic and cultural links.

Further reading

Enter the Vikings

The first permanent settlement on Iceland dates from 874, when Ingólfur Arnarson landed on the island. Two other journeys to the island before then are known about. One expedition for settlers ended in failure and a group of Irish monks lived on the island until the 9th century. This information is recorded in two unique medieval volumes: the *Íslendingabók* by Ari Þorgilsson, a summary of the history of Iceland from 874 to 1120, and the *Landnámabók* (The Settlement Book) by an unknown writer. This lists about 400 important settlement treks with the name of the leader.

During the 11th and 12th centuries, some 40 Icelandic sagas were recorded. In medieval times, these epic tales were highly regarded throughout Europe. Written in prose, some were based on oral traditions, most were works by unknown authors. The sagas look back over one to two centuries and describe events – often true – about important characters or clans in Iceland between 930 and 1030, a period known as the Saga Age. At the same time they served as propaganda, boosting the reputation of the island's elite.

Saga hero Grettir the Strong

The sagas possess a degree of authenticity not just with regard to the figures who feature in them, but also with regard to the customs and way of life at that time. As historical sources they continue to be of only limited value, although they did gain added authority when the Norwegian archaeologist, Helge Ingstad, used two of them to locate a Viking settlement on Canada's east coast. Excavations proved that Norsemen discovered America 500 years before Christopher Columbus... and you can read about it in the Greenland Saga and the Saga of Eric the Red. For centuries, nobody took the stories seriously.

Historical Highlights

Iceland is about 20 million years old. It continues to grow in size as a result of continued volcanic activity. The last Ice Age ended about 12,000 years ago.

AD225–305 Roman coins dating from this time found in southern and eastern Iceland. Historians are uncertain about their origin. Were Roman soldiers, perhaps blown off course, the first Europeans to land on Iceland or did later settlers bring the coins with them?

7th century Irish monks and the first Norse settlers arrive in Iceland.

793 The attack on the monastery at Lindisfarne off the coast of Northumberland in England marks the beginning of the Viking era.

874 Ingólfur Arnason, the 'First Settler', lands in a bay on the southwest coast, near the site of modern Reykavjík. Over the next decades, more settlers follow. Most of the new arrivals come from western Norway. About one in 10 originate from Norse settlements on the Scottish islands and Ireland. The reason for this immigration can be attributed to an expansionist Norwegian king to whom many clan leaders and landowners were unwilling to submit.

930 End of the 'Age of Settlement': Iceland's population is now about 25,000. All available land is divided up. The Icelandic Parliament, the Althing, is founded. Beginning of the Saga Age (until 1030).

1000 Discovery of North America by Leif Eriksson. Christianity is adopted as Iceland's official religion. The first bishopric is established in Skálholt in 1056, the second bishopric in Hólar in 1106.

1179 Birth of Snorri Sturluson, historian, diplomat and saga writer.

1241 Murder of Snorri Sturluson, by order of the King of Norway.

1262 Voluntary submission to the Norwegian crown, which from 1380 onwards rests on the heads of Danish monarchs.

16th century Hanseatic trading posts founded, e.g. in Hafnarfjörður (see page 25).

1541 Reformation in southern Iceland (Skálholt diocese) and in 1550 in northern Iceland (Hólar diocese).

1548 Catholic bishop Jón Arason leads a rebellion against the Protestants. Two years later King Christian III of Denmark orders his arrest. He is beheaded along with his two sons.

1602 Introduction of Danish trade monopoly, prohibiting Iceland from trading with any other countries. It remains in Danish hands until 1854.

1662 Absolute power throughout the whole Danish kingdom, Iceland included, until 1849.

1783–85 Eruption of the Laki crater (see page 47) decimates the population. The Danes consider resettling the 40,000 or so surviving Icelanders in Denmark.

1800 Abolition of the Althing on orders of the Danish king.

1814 At the end of the Napoleonic Wars Denmark loses Norway to archrivals Sweden, but retains power over the old Norwegian possessions of Iceland, Greenland and the Faroe Islands.

1843 Independence movement under Jón Sigurðsson (1811–79) brings about the re-instatement of the Althing.

1874 To celebrate the 1,000th anniversary of the settlement of the island, King Christian IX visits Iceland, the first Danish monarch to do so. He brings with him a new constitution, which from 1904 gives Iceland far-reaching autonomy in internal affairs.

1911 University established in Reykjavík.

1915 Iceland gets its own flag. Introduction of female suffrage for parliamentary elections.

1918 Union agreement with Denmark. The Danish king continues to be head of state, but the country is independent in every other respect.

1940 To protect Iceland from German occupation during World War II, British troops land on Iceland. Under a defence agreement, they are replaced in 1941 by Americans. Iceland is of great strategic importance in keeping Allied forces in the North Atlantic supplied.

1944 Iceland unilaterally withdraws from the union agreement with Denmark and becomes a republic on 17 June (National Independence Day).

1946 Iceland joins the United Nations. Start of commercial whaling.

1949 Despite strong popular resistance, Iceland abandons its neutrality and becomes a member of NATO. It does not have its own armed forces.

1951 The US military build the Keflavík airbase. It is still in use as a NATO base and international civilian airport.

1952 Extension of the fishery protection zone to 4 nautical miles. As with all subsequent extensions (1958 to 12 miles/19km, 1972 to 50 miles/80km, 1976 to 200 miles/320km), the decision meets with hostility from other fishing nations, mainly Great Britain (the Cod Wars).

1955 The Icelandic writer Halldór Laxness wins the Nobel Prize for Literature.

1963 The volcanic island of Surtsey emerges from the sea southwest of the Westman Islands.

1970 Iceland joins EFTA.

1973 A volcanic eruption forces the evacuation of Heimaey Island's 5,000 inhabitants (Westman Islands). Parts of the island's main town and harbour are saved by volunteers who manage to divert the lava flow.

1976 A 200-mile fishing limit off Iceland is agreed.

1980 Vigdis Finnbogadottir becomes president of Iceland – and the world's first democratically elected female head of state. She is re-elected three times, and holds office until 1996.

From 1984 Fishing quotas introduced to protect fish stocks in Icelandic waters.

1980 Vigdís Finnbogadóttir, the world's first democratically elected female head of state become president.

1985 Iceland ends commercial whaling. The controversial practice of 'scientific' whaling continues until 1989.

1986 Presidents Gorbachev and Reagan arrive in Reykjavík for a summit to start talks to end the Cold War.

1989 On Beer Day, 1 March, Icelanders celebrate the abolition, after a long campaign, of a ban on strong beer.

1992 Iceland leaves the International Whaling Commission after it rejects Iceland's request for a limited whaling quota. Iceland subsequently stops whaling, but does not declare itself a non-whaling country.

1994 Iceland enters the European Economic Area. In the disputed waters off Spitsbergen, Norwegian coastguards cut the nets of Icelandic trawlers using equipment that the Icelanders had developed for the Cod Wars (*see 1952 entry*).

1995 Heavy snowfalls in January and October result in the death of 34 people from avalanches.

1996 In September a volcano under the Vatnajökull ice-cap erupts. More than a month later, meltwater and ice floes as big as houses break out from under the ice (glacier burst) and wash 8km (5 miles) of Iceland's Ring Road into the sea. This was the only road link in southern Iceland (reopened in summer 1997).

1998 In December, the volcano under Vatnajökull erupts again, but there is no glacier burst.

2000 Iceland celebrates one thousand years of Christianity and Leifur Eriksson's discovery of North America in the year 1000. Reykjavík is voted a European City of Culture for the millennium. Mount Helka erupts on 26 February, and new lava stretches 3–4 km (2–3 miles). Several earthquakes hit the south of the island in June.

2001 Iceland joins the International Whaling Commission.

Route 1

Reykjavík

No smoke in 'Smoky Bay'

Reykjavík and the monument to Ingólfur Arnarson

As he approached Iceland for the first time, Ingólfur Arnarson, the country's first permanent settler, tossed his highseat pillars overboard, so that the gods could direct them to the settlement that they had chosen for him. The tree trunks, ornate with carvings, eventually found their way to a large bay in the southwest of Iceland, where steam from hot springs rose up into the air. Ingólfur called his new home 'Smoky Bay' or Reykjavík. In 1786 a town that

Café Paris

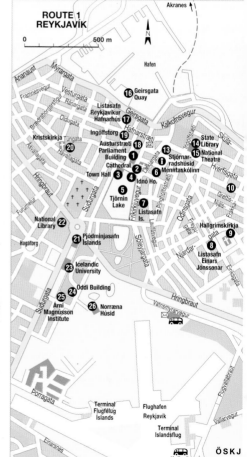

ROUTE 1
REYKJAVÍK

0   500 m

Akranes

Hafen

16 Geirsgata Quay

17 Listasafn Reykjavikur Hafnarhús

19 Ingólfstorg

18 Austurstræti

20 Kristkirkja

State Library 14

National Theatre 15

13 Stjórnarradshúsid

6 Menntaskólinn

Parliament Building 1

Cathedral 2

Town Hall 3

Idnó Ho. 4

5

7 Listasafn Ís.

Tjörnin Lake

22 National Library

21 Pjódminjasafn Íslands

Hagatorg

23 Icelandic University

24 Oddi Building

25 Árni Magnusson Institute

26 Norræna Húsid

Hallgrímskirkja 8

9

Listasafn Einars Jónssonar

Hringbraut

Terminal Flugfélag Íslands

Flughafen Reykjavik

Terminal Islandsflug

Keflavik   ÖSKJ

Preceding pages: Gullfoss

had barely 200 inhabitants won its municipal charter. However appropriate it may have seemed to Ingólfur, the name 'Smoky Bay' is now a long way from the truth. Apart from motor vehicle exhausts, Reykjavík is effectively a smoke-free zone. All of the houses in the town of 109,000 inhabitants, together with its suburbs where another 65,000 people live, are heated with geothermal energy. From the numerous vantage points around the city, the air above the colourful roofs of this modern, spacious capital always looks fresh and clear.

Two circular tours for visitors to sample the atmosphere and to identify the main places of interest in the Icelandic capital can easily be completed on foot. For the third tour, however, some form of transport is recommended.

Feeding the birds

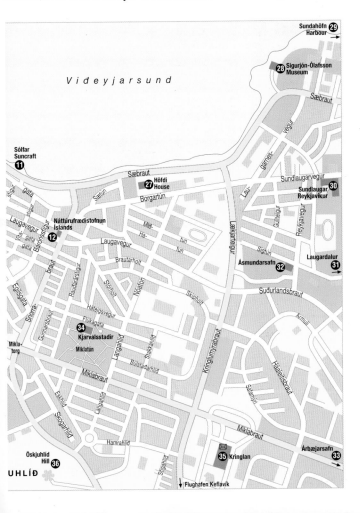

A tour through the city centre

To obtain a good first impression of the city, start this circular tour at the tourist office at Bankstræti 2 where up-to-date information *is available. Overlooking Austurvöllur Square is the **Parliament Building ❶**, the Althing, the oldest parliament in the world. After centuries in Þingvellir *(see page 66)*, it was *moved to Reykjavík in 1845 and then installed in its present premises in 1881, when the island was still under Danish rule, as is clear from the royal coat-of-arms of Christian IX above the doorway.

In the middle of Austurvöllur stands a statue of the father of independent Iceland, Jón Sigurðsson *(see page 60)*. A font in front of the altar of the rather plain **Cathedral ❷**, situated on the east side of the square, is the work of Bertel Thorvaldsen. The Dane with an Icelandic father was one of the most important sculptors of the 19th-century neoclassical era.

The Town Hall

The Icelandic parliament building looks small when compared to the bold **Town Hall ❸**, which was completed in 1992. Because of the shortage of space in the central area, it was built on water reclaimed from Tjörnin Lake. The spiralling costs for this building were a source of controversy. A large relief map of Iceland can be viewed in the basement.

A footbridge links the Town Hall with **Idnó House ❹**, a timber construction dating from the beginning of the 20th century. It is now a cultural centre and theatre.

Tjörnin Lake

Tjörnin Lake ❺, a peaceful haven in the heart of the city, is well known for its rich bird life. From the northeast corner ★ **Menntaskólinn ❻**, the long-established grammar school, is visible above Lækjargata. Before 1847 it was the only school in the country that offered pupils a route to university, usually one in Denmark.

★★ **Listasafn Íslands ❼**, the National Art Gallery (Fríkirkjuvegur 7), is set in the architecturally effective combination of an old ice warehouse and a light and airy, modern structure. It is used primarily for temporary exhibitions of new and contemporary Icelandic art. Visitors may well be tempted by the café on the first floor (Tuesday to Sunday 11am–5pm).

Hallgrímskirkja

Pass through the smart residential district of Reykjavík with its many diplomatic residences and then up to the Hallgrimskirkja church. Directly in front of it is **Listasafn Einars Jónssonar ❽** (Njarðargata), a museum in the former home and studio of the sculptor Einar Jónsson (1874–1954). A cross-section of his work, much of which depicts mythological and religious symbolism, is in the sculpture garden behind (garden: daily 11am–4pm).

The ★★ **Hallgrímskirkja ❾** was designed by Guðjón Samúelsson (1887–1950), for many years the national

The Sólfar Suncraft

architect. Dominating the city centre, it can be seen from many miles away. It was finally consecrated in 1987 after a 40-year construction period. The exterior is reminiscent of Icelandic basalt rock formations, while the airy interior with its tall, slender concrete columns has a distinctive Gothic look.

21

Equipped with an enormous ★ 72-register German organ and 5,275 pipes, the Hallgriímskirkja is noted for its fine acoustics. The highlight of the church, however, is the 75-m (245-ft) high platform in the tower, which offers the best possible view over Reykjavík (viewing platform: daily in summer 9am–6pm, winter 10am–5pm).

Several routes lead from the church to **Laugavegur ⑩**, a busy shopping street. Geothermal underfloor heating keeps the pavements free of snow and ice during the winter. The international designer fashion shops in Laugavegur, Bankastræti and Hverfisgata offer particularly good value as a 15 percent VAT reduction is available to foreign visitors *(see page 92)*. The same applies to the elegant jewellery and superior-quality clocks and watches.

Top brands on Laugavegur

The Icelandic Phallological Museum (Laugavegur 24; summer Tuesday to Saturday 2–5pm, winter Tuesday and Saturday 2–5pm) has a *collection – the only one of its kind in the world – of over 60 penises and penal parts belonging to almost all the land and sea mammals that can be found in Iceland, plus other phallic objects.

Reaching the parts other museums don't

Take a detour from here to the **Sólfar Suncraft ⑪** on the banks of the Viðeyjarsund. This modern work of art made of stainless steel by Gunnar Árnason (1931–89) was built in 1986. Come and enjoy Iceland's romantic sunsets at this waterside spot.

A little further to the west along Laugavegur is the tourist information office; follow the road to the east and you come to Hlemmur Square and the **Náttúrufrædistofnun Íslands ⑫**, Iceland's Natural History Museum.

Live music at the Ingólfstorg

*National Theatre (above) and
the Stjórnarráðshúsið*

From the city centre to the university quarter

Opposite the tourist information office stands the **Stjórnarráðshúsið ⑬**, built during the colonial era as a prison but now used as the offices of the Icelandic prime minister. Make the short detour to the north to Arnarhóll and the **monument to Ingólfur Arnarson**, Iceland's first settler, then take a few steps into Hverfisgata to the building where the **State Library ⑭** was housed and which is now *an art and cultural centre. The **National Theatre ⑮** is another striking concrete building by Guðjón Samúelsson.

More and more cruise ships now call in at Reykjavík and they moor at the **Geirsgata quay ⑯**. Directly opposite *the quay, in the Tollhúsip (Tryggvagata 19), there is a good chance of a bargain at the **Kolaportið Flea Market** (Saturday and Sunday 11am–5pm). At Tryggvagata 17 is **Listasafn Reykjavíkur Hafnarhús ⑰**, the Reykjavik Art Museum (daily 11am–6pm, until 7pm on Thurs). Follow the traffic-calmed **Austurstræti ⑱** shopping street to the modern **Ingólfstorg ⑲**, built in 1994. This is often the venue on Sundays for cultural events. Later in the evening it becomes a lively meeting place for skaters and motorcyclists.

Carved falcons on the roof ridges of the Falcon House on the north side of the Ingólfstorg serve as a reminder of this building's original function. During the colonial era gerfalcons from all over the country were collected here before being presented to the European aristocracy as gifts from the Danish king.There is plenty of activity late in the evening when live music is performed in the **Fógetinn** (Apalstræti 10), a pub that occupies the oldest house in the inner city.

Túngata climbs the hill to the Catholic **Kristskirkja ⑳**. Before the Hallgrímskirkja was completed, this was the largest church in the city, even though the number of Icelanders who are Catholics is less than 1 percent.

On the way to the university quarter you will pass the

★ **Þjóðminjasafn Íslands** ㉑ (Suðurgata 41; Tuesday to Sunday 11am–5pm), the National Museum. Exhibits in this recently renovated building include art, handicrafts and tools from the Viking era. On the other side of the road stands a distinctive, modern building, known to the locals as the 'book castle'. Iceland's **National Library** (Landsbókasafn Íslands Haskólabókasafn) ㉒ does indeed look like a fortified building. Housed under one roof are both the National Library and the University Library. The **Icelandic University** (Háskóli Íslands) ㉓ moved into the main block in 1940. Now this seat of learning with nine faculties has just under 6,000 students. To find out what life is like in an Icelandic University, enter the **Oddi Building** ㉔ and view the university's art collection in the corridor. The collection of world-famous saga manuscripts is kept in the ★ **Árni Magnússon Institute** ㉕, another university building (summer Monday to Saturday 11am–4pm; winter Tuesday to Friday 2–4pm).

The Icelandic University

On your way back to the city centre, stop off for a refreshment break at the cafeteria in the **Norræna Húsið** ㉖. This cultural exhibition centre, opened in 1968, was a gift from the Scandinavian nations for the promotion of cultural exchanges. It is just one of the fine public buildings designed by the top Finnish architect, Alvar Aalto.

23

Culture and relaxation among the hot springs

This circular tour can be completed on foot, but it passes through some suburban areas and industrial zones where there is little of interest. Rather than walk the whole way, a bicycle or a car would be more suitable.

Start out from Hlemmur Square by the **Natural History Museum** *(see page 21)*. Students of modern history will be familiar with the rôle played by the **Höfði House** ㉗. It was here in 1986 where Mikhail Gorbachev and Ronald Reagan met for their first superpower summit – which marked the beginning of the end of the Cold War.

The **Sigurjón-Ólafsson Museum** ㉘ (Laugarnestangi 70) pays homage to the painter and sculptor Sigurjón Ólafsson (1908–82). He used mainly materials that the sea deposited outside his studio and which he then collected as he strolled along the shoreline. The museum is situated by the sea and the view from the museum across his sculptures by the shore and sweeping out over the Atlantic is stunning. Every Tuesday during the summer evening concerts are performed here against the background of the setting sun (1 June–31 August Tuesday–Sunday 2–5pm, otherwise Saturday and Sunday 2–5pm).

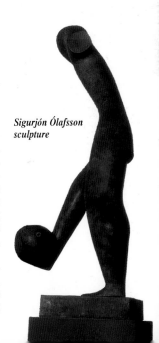

Sigurjón Ólafsson sculpture

A boat leaves regularly from a jetty in the commercial **Sundahöfn harbour** ㉙ to the island of ★ **Viðey**. Only a few overgrown remains from the herb garden have survived from the medieval Augustinian monastery, but

The Sundlaugar Reykjavíkur

The Botanical Gardens

Perlan

Viðeyarstofa House is Iceland's oldest stone building. It was restored in the 1980s and now houses a **gourmet restaurant** (tel: 568 1045; $$$). On the west side of the island a circular walk takes in a piece of landscape art by Richard Serra, known as *Stages*.

No one should leave Reykjavík without visiting one of the swimming pools. The city's largest pool is ★ **Sundlaugar Reykjavíkur ㉚** (Sundlaugarvegur; Monday–Friday 7am–9.30pm, Saturday and Sunday 8am–7.30pm). It is situated to the east of the city centre in Laugardalur. *Do relax in one of the hot pots (geothermal hot tub), but don't make the mistake of jumping into the emptiest one: it will almost certainly be the hottest, at around 45°C (113°F). Start in the coolest pot, which will be about 37°C (98°F).

Further up in **Laugardalur ㉛**, the **Botanical Gardens** give a detailed and informative background to Iceland's flora. Children will appreciate the adjoining **zoo**. Most of the animals are domesticated, but there are birds, seals and reindeer. There is also a **playground** for children.

On the way back to the city there is another opportunity to absorb Icelandic art and culture. ★ **Ásmundarsafn ㉜** (Sigtún 5; 1 May–30 September, daily 10am–4pm, otherwise daily 1–4pm; the sculpture park is always open) is a museum dedicated to the work of Ásmundur Sveinsson, without doubt Iceland's most famous sculptor.

Off the beaten track

★★ **Árbæjarsafn ㉝** in the suburb of Árbær is an open-air museum with a collection of mainly rural, but also urban buildings from the past two centuries. They are often used as settings for demonstrations of old craft skills. Open summer Tuesday–Friday 9am–5pm, Saturday and Sunday 10am–6pm; bus 10/110 from the city centre.

Kjarvalsstaðir ㉞ (Flókagata 9; open daily 10am–6pm, until 7pm on Wednesday), the municipal art museum, has a wide collection by Iceland's most famous painters, Jóhannes S. Kjarval (1885–1972) and Erró (b. 1932). Temporary exhibitions are also held alongside their work.

Kringlan ㉟, a super-modern shopping arcade, is the centre of a purpose-built complex. As well as small shops and supermarkets, this is where visitors will find one of the legendary Hard Rock cafés. On view are rock memorabilia. On sale are Hard Rock T-shirts and sweatshirts.

The heating and hot water for the city of Reykjavík used to be collected in five huge tanks on **Öskjuhlíð hill ㊱** on the eastern edge of the city airport. Mounted on the tanks is ★ **Perlan**, the 'Pearl', a glass dome visible from miles away. On the top floor beneath Perlan, a luxury restaurant rotates on its own axis once every hour (tel: 562 0200; $$$). Less expensive is the cafeteria on the floor below, with access to a viewing platform and magnificent views.

Excursions from Reykjavík

Look out to the southwest from any of the vantage points in Reykjavík and you are bound to see a free-standing, gleaming white building. **Bessastaðir** on the Álftanes promontory is the residence of the head of state. Since the Middle Ages this has been the home of Iceland's most powerful and important figures. One resident was Snorri Sturluson, the Edda author.

★ **Hafnarfjörður**, Reykjavík's neighbour to the south, has not been overwhelmed by the capital's suburbs and has managed to retain its independence. The centre of the town lies beside the fine natural harbour, which made the place very attractive to merchants from northern Germany during the period of Hanseatic trade. Situated by the harbour now is ★ **Sjóminjasafn Íslands** (Vesturgata 8), Iceland's Maritime Museum. Right next to it is **Byggðasafn Hafnarfjarðar**, the Municipal Museum, where a collection of cultural and historical artefacts is kept. The two buildings and the romantic **Restaurant A. Hansen** (Vesturgata 4; tel: 565 1130; $$$) make an attractive ensemble of 19th-century houses. **Hafnarborg** (Strandgata 34) is an artistic and cultural centre often used for exhibitions.

Hafnarfjörður's Municipal Museum

25

At some time visitors to the town should take a trip round the **Hellisgerði** lava park, a green area in a bizarre tract of lava, which can easily be imagined as the home of elves and trolls. Hafnarfjörður likes to describe itself as the capital of their kingdom.

Suðurnes, Iceland's southwestern peninsula, often known as **Reykjanes**, is the site of Keflavík international airport, the gateway to Iceland. It is this part of the country that most new arrivals first see and many of them get quite a shock. The journey from Keflavík to Reykjavík passes through some particularly barren countryside. But then this peninsula can boast some spectacular coastline, mainly to the south and southwest. The area is especially popular with birdwatchers at migration time.

The Blue Lagoon

★★ **Bláa Lonið** (Blue Lagoon), to the north of the fishing village of Grindavík, is one of Iceland's principal attractions. In 1999 the bathing facilities were moved to a new and extravagantly designed site in the heart of a bizarre lava field. The pool is fed by a constant supply of warm water (40°C/104°F) rich in silica, salt and other elements. The on-site clinic uses the special healing powers of the water to successfully treat the skin complaint, psoriasis. The salty water emerges from a borehole 1,500m (5,000ft) deep. Only after the water has passed through a heat exchanger and supplied energy to a power station and a heating system is the temperature cool enough for the bathers. For further details, tel: 420 8800; fax: 420 8801; web: www.bluelagoon.is).

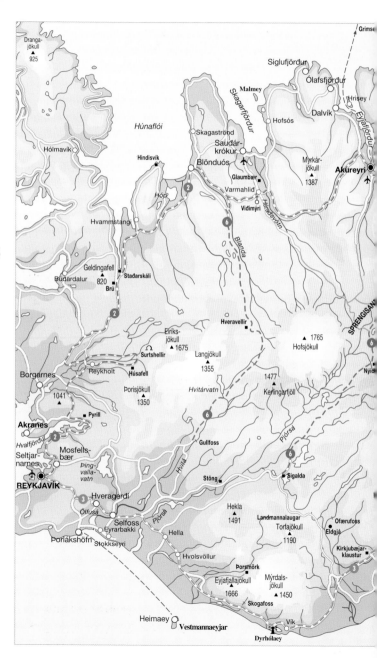

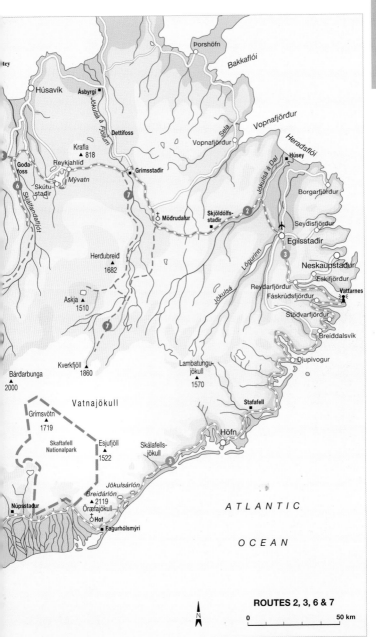

ROUTES 2, 3, 6 & 7

0   50 km

N

Volcanic landscapes and forms at Jökulsárgljúfur National Park

Route 2

Along the Ring Road through Iceland's west and north

Reykjavík – Húsafell – Akureyri – Goðafoss – Mývatn – Egilsstaðir (775km/480 miles) *See map on page 26*

Apart from just one or two detours, this route follows the northern half of the Ring Road on its way to Akureyri, the largest town in Iceland outside the greater Reykjavík area, and passes close to deeply-carved fjords and broad bays. Beyond this important staging post lie the famous Goðafoss waterfall and Mývatn Lake, a paradise for bird-watchers. This is where Mother Earth has created an open-air volcanology museum. The further you penetrate into the northeast, the lonelier, the more inhospitable and the more fascinating the landscape becomes.

You should set aside at least three days for this route. If possible, allow longer for the Mývatn region. A bus service operates from Reykjavík to Akureyri and on to Egilsstaðir, following the Ring Road and this route.

Þyrill mountain in winter

Leave **Reykjavík** through the suburb of **Mosfellsbær**. Some of Reykjavík's hot water comes from the geothermal springs here. The long **Hvalfjörður** or 'Whale Fjord' can be reached from the foot of the 909-m (2,982-ft) high Mount Esja, where during the winter there is good skiing on the eastern slopes. The Ring Road follows the tunnel, completed in 1998, under the inlet (toll charge ISK 1,000), but Route 2 follows Highway 47 around the fjord. Overlooking the northern shores is **Þyrill** mountain, the setting for an exciting episode in one of the Settlement-era sagas. The daughter of one of the chieftains saves herself and her sons from pirates after a daring escape up the mountain. A little further along beside the fjord is Iceland's only remaining **whaling station**, but it is currently not in service.

Near the Ferstikla roadside service area (81km/50 miles), Route 2 leaves the Ring Road and follows Highways 50 and 518 to **Reykholt** (124km/77 miles). This was the home of Snorri Sturluson (1206–41), the outstanding man of letters of medieval Scandinavia and powerful chieftain who was assassinated at the behest of the king of Norway. His monument, created by Gustav Vigeland in 1947, stands in front of the old school building. Excavations in Reykolt have uncovered a number of medieval foundations, including Snorri's bathing pool.

It is definitely worth stopping to see **Hraunfossar** or 'Lava Waterfall' (143km/88 miles), situated some way inland. A small river flows underground above impermeable strata up to the bank of a larger river. Water bubbles out from the lava across a wide expanse between moss, grass and shrubs.

Visitors to Hraunfossar

Húsafell (148km/91 miles) is a popular holiday destination for Icelanders. Many summer homes nestle in a small birch wood. The settlement is a good starting point for excursions into the Arnarvatnsheiði walking area. In summer snowmobiles leave a mountain cabin 18km (11 miles) southeast of Húsafell for the ice-cap of the 1,400-m (4,600-ft) high Langjökull. Daily excursions are also organised from Reykjavík. For more information and reservations contact Langjökull ehf, tel: 567 1205.

Highway 518 swings round in a broad curve close to the uninhabited uplands and then heads west, affording some incredible views over the dome-shaped **Eiríksjökull** ice-cap. Near the Fljótstunga farmstead (154km/95 miles), a track forks off to the Surtshellir and Stefánshellir lava caves (guided tours from Húsafell). Shortly before the Ring Road (203km/125 miles), a side road leads to the educational and agricultural centre at **Varmaland**. As well as boasting a thermal bath, there are some small shops where locally grown produce is sold.

Aspects of Húsafell

It is worth making the arduous climb through the cinders to the **Grábrók** crater (216km/134 miles) for the view alone. The road climbs slowly but steadily to Holtavörðuheiði at an altitude of over 400m (1,300ft). In severe winters the Ring Road in this highland valley can be blocked off by snow for days. At these times northern and southern Iceland are linked only by air or by sea.

For over a hundred years travellers have interrupted their journey in **Staðarskáli**, (274km/170 miles), which lies about halfway between Reykjavík and Akureyri, the two most important population centres in Iceland. A primitive coaching station during the 19th century, the settlement

has become a modern staging post, which has even been the subject for poetry and songs. Staðarskáli is now almost a synonym for a roadside service area.

The **Reykir** education centre (288km/178 miles) lies below the Ring Road beside Hrútafjörður, an arm of Húnaflói bay and formerly a centre for Icelandic shark fishing, the main theme of Reykir's local history museum.

A detour to **Hvammstangi** (302km/187 miles) starts just past **Laugarbakki**. The 75-km (45-mile) long road hugs the coast of the Vatnsnes peninsula. **Hamarsrétt** seaside sheep-fold, where in autumn local farmers meet to sort out ownership of the sheep and horses, **Hindisvík** seal bay almost at the northern tip of the peninsula and, on its eastern shores, **Hvítserkur**, a rock shrouded in legend resembling a petrified dragon, are the main highlights along this stretch. The coast road meets up with the Ring Road near **Bogarvirki**, the only medieval fortress on Iceland. This is no powerful fortification, but some unspectacular walls reinforce this natural hide-out on the crest of a hill.

Hindisvík seal bay and Hvítserkur rock

Hóp is a tidal lake, which increases in size by about a third at high tide. The small stone church of Þingeyrar on the eastern shore marks the spot where one of Iceland's most important spiritual centres, a Benedictine monastery, stood during the Middle Ages. In the Skagafjörður hinterland, a lane leads to the turf-covered church of **Viðimyri**, which dates from 1834. The nearby settlement of **Varmahlíð** (405km/251 miles) near hot springs can provide travellers with fuel, roadside services, a supermarket with tourist information in summer, a hotel, a post office and, of course, a swimming pool.

Viðimyri church

While the Ring Road crosses the barren 535-m (1,755-ft) high **Öxnadalsheiði**, before descending to the slender **Hraundrangar** rocky spire (1,075m/3,526ft) and **Eyjafjörður** within easy reach of **Akureyri**, Varmahlíð marks the starting point for a number of diversions and detours of various lengths.

The ★★ **Glaumbær Folk Museum** lies about 7km (4 miles) north of Varmahlíð on Highway 75. The former vicarage is a typical example of the building style adopted in rural areas before the dawn of the 20th century. The central section consists of adjoining turf-covered houses, each with only one room. Despite the size of the farm, living accommodation was very cramped, as is clear from the *baðstofa*, the largest room in Glaumbær. Not only did up to 22 people sleep on the 11 beds, many also had to work sitting on them.

The Skagafjörður region is famous throughout Iceland for horse breeding. In the latter part of September, the animals are all brought down from the upland summer pastures for winter. If you are in the area at this time of year, be sure not to miss this colourful event *(see page 75)*.

Sauðárkrókur was founded in the late 19th century. This town, which now has a population of about 3,000, is the second most important settlement in northern Iceland after Akureyri. One major attraction is the boat excursions to the rocky island of **Drangey**, which juts out from the water in striking fashion. In the spring, it is a favourite haunt of puffins.

Between the years 1106 and 1810 **Hólar** was, after Skálholt, Iceland's second diocese. It was from here that the forces of Catholicism in Scandinavia made their last stand against the Reformation. Bishop Jón Arason stood up to the new movement sweeping Europe and became a folk hero until he and two of his two sons paid with their lives for their obstinacy *(see page 64)*. Iceland's only Baroque sandstone church, consecrated in 1763, is a reminder of more illustrious times. An agricultural college, which doubles in the summer as a tourist information office, a basic hostel and a cafeteria, dominates the town.

Life on the range

31

Hofsós museum

There is an impressive coastal landscape to appreciate between **Hofsós** – with its restored trading post dating from the Danish Trade Monopoly (1777), now a local history museum and the Icelandic Emigration Museum (Vesturfarasafnið á Hofsósi) – and the former herring capital of **Siglufjörður**. The local museum is unique – it is the only one in the world that focuses exclusively on the herring. Every year in the second half of July a festival recalls the fish that once brought riches to the town.

A short pass cuts through from Siglufjörður to the western shores of the pretty Eyjafjörður inlet, the fishing villages of **Ólafsfjörður** and **Dalvík** and finally Akureyri.

Landscape near Siglufjörður

Akureyri's botanical gardens

Akureyri

This small town (500km/310 miles), which likes to describe itself as the capital of northern Iceland, is home to just under 15,000 inhabitants. It is the largest town in the country outside the metropolitan area of Reykjavík and the fourth largest in Iceland. Its role as the focus for a large part of the island is evident from its numerous cultural and educational institutions. Akureyri has Iceland's second university, a theatre, a number of museums, good sporting facilities, a large airport and enough hotels and restaurants to cope with the summer influx of tourists.

One of the first settlers in the 10th century was Helgi Magri or Helgi the Lean. A memorial to him on the northern edge of the town centre makes an excellent viewpoint.

The town first came to prominence in 1602 when it was an outpost for the Danish Trade Monopoly. In 1862 the town with its 256 inhabitants was granted its municipal charter. After World War II Akureyri underwent a period of growth and a lot of new buildings sprang up around the small town centre. The port, a popular stopping-off point for North Atlantic cruises, is the hub of economic activity. The processing of fish and agricultural products provide employment as do a chocolate factory and a brewery.

Tour of the museums and a garden

Starting from the tourist information office near the **bus station** ❶, make for the theatre, which is housed in an attractive timber construction dating from the beginning of the 20th century. Then pass the oldest house in the town, the Laxdalshús (Hafnarstræti 11; 1795), and continue as far as Aðalstræti. Next to one another there are the **Regional Museum** (Minjasafnið) ❷ with a collection of artefacts of cultural and historic interest (summer daily 11am–5pm, winter Sunday 2–4pm) and the **Nonnahús Memorial Museum** ❸. It was here where Reverend Jón 'Nonni' Sveinsson spent five years of his childhood (1 June–15 September, daily 10am–5pm). Sveinsson wrote a series of books for children about a boy called Nonni growing up in the north of Iceland. Originally written in German, they were later translated into about 40 languages.

When returning to the town centre, call in at the ★ **Botanical Gardens** (Lystigarðurinn) ❹, probably the most northerly gardens in the world. At any rate, this site must be Iceland's most attractive garden. Nearly all the country's plants as well as many species from other countries are grown here

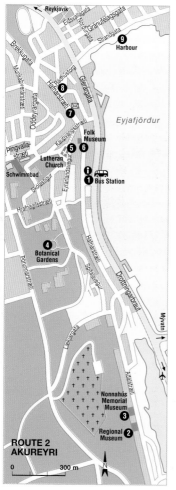

Reykjavik
Eldsvallagata
Grænufélagsgata
Strandgata
❾ Harbour
Brekkugata
Munkaþverárstræti
Oddeyrargata
Hafnarstræti
Hafnarstóp
Glerárgata
❽
✉
❼
Eyjafjörður
Kaupvangsstræti
Folk Museum
❺ ❻
Þingvalla-stræti
Lutheran Church
Skólastígur
Schwimmbad
ℹ 🚌
❶ Bus Station
Eyrarlandsvegur
Hrafnagilsstræti
❹ Botanical Gardens
Hafnarstræti
Spítalavegur
Drottningarbraut
Byggðavegur
Myvatn
Laxagata
† † †
† † †
† † † †
† † † †
Nonnahús
† † † Memorial
† † † Museum
Aðalstræti
❸
ROUTE 2
AKUREYRI
Regional ❷ Museum
0   300 m   N

under the theme of 'Arctic Flora' (daily 9am–10pm).

After Einar Jónsson's sculpture *The Outlaw*, a figure looking out towards the fjord with his child on his arm and his (dead) wife over his shoulders, you will come to the main **Lutheran church** (daily 9.30–11am and 2–3pm), consecrated in 1940. The centre window in the chancel originally graced Coventry Cathedral.

A flight of steps leads from the church's main entrance down to the town centre, where it joins Kaupvangsstræti, known locally as **Listagil** ('Arts Gorge'). At the beginning of the 1990s, some older industrial properties were converted into an interesting collection of studios and meeting rooms, plus Akureyri Art Gallery.

Instead of touring Akureyri's old buildings and modern churches, you may prefer to pay a visit to the town's swimming pool, which is well supplied with hot pots, plus a large fun slide. It is situated in Þingvallastræti above the 'Arts Gorge'.

Return to the bus station and the tourist information office, situated past the **Folk Museum** (Náttúrugripasafnid)  (Hafnarstræti 81; 1 June–15 September, daily 10am–5pm, otherwise Sunday 1–4pm). It claims to have examples of all birds that nest in Iceland and is also well regarded as a research centre into lichens and fungi.

The northern section of **Hafnarstræti**, now a pedestrian zone, is the town's main shopping street and this leads on to **Rádhústorg** or Town Hall Square. On weekend evenings the young people of Akureyri pay homage to America's cultural influence by ostentatiously cruising round here in their cars. It is only a few metres from here to the **harbour** and Strandgata, where the cruise ships moor during the summer.

Brekkugata, a northward extension of Hafnarstræti, runs north past the sports ground and on to the Helgi Magri memorial *(see page 32)*, worth a visit for the view alone.

Akureyri viewed from the eastern shore of the fjord

33

The Lutheran church

Godafoss

Laufás local history museum

Just south of Akureyri, bridges and causeways carry the main road to the east over the end of Eyjafjörður. The Ring Road then runs along its eastern shores. Initially there are some great views of Akureyri and then of the fjord as the road heads north. Before you turn to the east through a pass down into the Fnjóská valley, take a detour of 12km (7 miles) to the **Laufás** local history museum, which occupies an old vicarage. The turf-covered building was constructed between 1840 and 1866. Some 13 living rooms and communal areas, as well as the timber church, which dates from 1865, are open to the public (beginning of June–mid-September, daily except Monday 10am–6pm)

★ **Godafoss** or 'Waterfall of the Gods' (549km/341 miles) does not fall a great distance but it is an amazing sight as rocks split up the surging water flow of the Skjálfandafljót river into several sections. The name derives from the early Christian era when a local chieftain threw carvings of the Norse gods into the river.

At the Arctic Circle on Grimsey

Unlike many of the offshore islands, **Grímsey**, about 40km (25 miles) from the mainland to the north of Akureyri is inhabited. About 100 people, including youngsters, earn a living from the still well-stocked fishing grounds. Before a telephone line was laid in 1931, a supply boat called in twice a year with provisions. Now there is a runway and a Twin Otter can fly from Akureyri in about 20 minutes.

Grímsey is the only part of Iceland on the Arctic Circle (66° 30' N). Birding enthusiasts come to see the plentiful puffins and the rarer little auk. **Básar** (tel: 467 3103) can offer beds, space for sleeping bags and simple meals.

Laugar (558km/346 miles) is not an attraction in itself but it does make a good alternative base for exploring the Myvatn region about 30km (19 miles) away.

Lake Myvatn

Soon after Laugar the road reaches a small lake (573km/ 356 miles), set amid a barren landscape. Tour guides relate the story of some Americans who returned a hire car to Akureyri, complaining about how boring Mývatn was, but the mileometer revealed that the vehicle had barely come as far as this lake, the Másvatn. It is only beyond the next range of hills that ★★★ **Lake Mývatn** comes into view. Initially, you will encounter its outflow, the Laxá (578km/359 miles), a river famous for its salmon and trout, and notorious for the extortionate cost of fishing permits. The river is the preferred breeding-ground for the harlequin duck and the Barrow's goldeneye duck, two species that have arrived here from America. This is the only European breeding area for the latter species.

Mývatn means the 'midge lake'. The evidence for this is clearly visible on windless days in June and August – less so in July – when swarms of these tiny flies swirl above the water close to the shore. They are, of course, a vital source of food for the lake's bird life. One consolation is that very few of the flies are biters; the female blackfly, which only lives by the banks of the Laxá, bites

Light show on Lake Mývatn

ROUTE 2
MYVATN

0   2 km

Dimmuborgir

Seljahjallagil textures

humans. Nevertheless, the non-biting majority certainly make their presence felt. They exist in such numbers that they penetrate into the nose, the eyes, even the ears.

The Ring Road soon reaches **Skútustaðir** (587km/364 miles) and the protected ★★ **Skútustaðagígar** pseudo-crater at the edge of the lake. Many years ago molten lava flowed over the damp terrain, trapped steam exploded and the lava crust burst open. Pseudocraters have no connection with the volcanic pipe.

One of the most attractive spots by Mývatn is **Höfdi** woodland park (594km/369 miles), set on a spit jutting out into the lake. Compared to the rest of Iceland with its bleak landscape, this green corner is like a primeval forest. The view from Höfdi extends out over the lake taking in the bizarre lava pillars, for a long time now distinctive symbols for Lake Mývatn.

Mother Earth also created some bizarre shapes at **Dimmuborgir** ('Twilight Castles'; 596km/370 miles and then another 2km/1¼ miles to the car park). Onlookers will inevitably allow their imagination to run riot in search of some of mystical explanation for these weird shapes. Who built these castle towers, the cathedral, the bridges, the ramparts and the dungeons? The scientific background is quite simple: Dimmuborgir was formed when the Prengslaborgir series of craters further east erupted. An obstacle caused the molten lava to form into a lake, which then cooled unevenly. Eventually the blockage gave way and the lava that was still in liquid form flowed away leaving behind these 'Twilight Castles'.

The prominent and evenly formed tephra gravel ring, **Hverfell** (597km/370 miles), has nothing to do with molten lava. Standing a good 180m (590ft) above the surrounding terrain, it can easily be reached on foot (about 2km/1¼ miles) by someone in good shape – a worthwhile, if dusty, experience. It is a much longer walk to the **Lúdent**, Hverfell's counterpart. Both of these are the result of short but very violent eruptions. **Lúdentsborgir** and **Prengslaborgir**, a series of craters to the south, are also examples of this type of volcano.

You have to pass this way to get to one of the most mysterious sites in the region, the 60-m (196-ft) deep basalt-pillared gorge of ★ **Seljahjallagil**. Although it is in ecological terms a very sensitive area, the gorge is open to tourism. It can be reached as part of a day hike, but visitors are requested to be very careful. It is also possible to explore the gorge under expert guidance as part of a tour starting in Reykjahlíd.

Reykjahlíd (600km/372 miles) is the main tourist centre for Lake Mývatn. The huge plates of lava which surround the village, and the village church in particular, make a fascinating sight. The previous church was miraculously spared during the Great Mývatn Fire (1724–29). Because it stood on a low and barely perceptible rise, the flow parted and missed the church by only a few metres. Other examples of volcanic phenomena are the hot-spring caves at **Stóragjá**, situated beside the Ring Road, and **Grjótagjá**, beside a track a few kilometres to the southwest. Dramatic changes in water temperature have occurred in past years as a result of activity way below the earth's surface.

It you are unsure whether it is safe to bathe in one of the caves, seek advice locally. But remember that if you do bathe in one of these naturally heated pools, you will be swimming in warm, unchlorinated water after hundreds of other bathers. A much more hygienic option is to pay a visit to the modern thermal baths with some relaxing hot pots situated at the eastern end of Reykjahlíd.

Grazing near the lake

The next section of this route as far as Egilsstadir is often closed in winter. There's a good chance of snow from mid-September until well into May. On the outskirts of Reykjahlíd is a factory that uses geothermal energy to process the diatoms in Lake Mývatn's sediment into diatomite, a raw material used in industrial filters, insulating materials and cosmetics. The removal of the minuscule diatoms is a controversial issue; environmentalists suspect that the lake's bird population will be endangered.

37

At the foot of ★ **Námaskard** (605km/375 miles) lies **Hverarönd**, one of Iceland's best-known geothermal fields, with sulphur deposits and a series of mud pots and steam vents. During the colonial era, the Danish kings extracted sulphur for gunpowder here. It is a sensible idea to wrap plastic bags around your shoes as the mud near the springs is sticky and difficult to scrape off.

A side road (7km/4 miles) off the solfatara field opposite goes to **Krafla** and its explosion crater known as Víti

Mud pot at Námaskard

Dettifoss

('Hell'). A power station there converts energy from the earth's core into electricity. New fields of lava formed during the middle of the 1980s are open to the public. The whole area is volcanically active and walkers should check the notice boards for up-to-date information.

Just under 30km (19 miles) north of **Grímsstaðir** (campsite; 639km/397 miles) is ★★ **Dettifoss** *(see page 39)*, a waterfall definitely worth the detour, even though Highway 864 is only a very rough track.

There is a longer, alternative route for the stretch between Reykjahlíð and Grímsstaðir (an additional 145km/90 miles and at least one extra day). Leave the Mývatn region in a northerly direction towards Húsavík. Just off the main road is the **Grenjaðarstaður Folk Museum** in a turf-covered farmhouse that dates from the mid-19th century.

Húsavík (pop. 2,500) is an important town in this part of northern Iceland. It was catapulted on to the world map in 1995 as Iceland's 'whale watch' capital. During the summer the waters off Húsavík swarm with whales and it is possible to go on ★★ **whale-sighting excursions** which are almost guaranteed success. Occasionally, even blue whales are sighted; and in August the impressive humpback whales appear in these waters, too.

Whale-sighting

An informative **Whale Centre** has been set up in Húsavík harbour. It doubles as a tourist information centre (tel: 464 2520, fax: 464 2161; May–September, daily 10am–10pm).

Two companies now take whale enthusiasts out to sea in search of these great mammals – sometimes as many as nine times a day. Norður Sigling (tel: 464 2350, 3 hours, about £25) has two beautifully restored oak cutters which are ideal for such excursions, while the other company, Sjóferðir Arnars (tel: 464 1748, 3 hours, about £22) uses a larger converted steel cutter for the whale excursions.

Húsavík, meaning 'House Bay', likes to describe itself as the first Norse settlement on Iceland. According to old manuscripts, Garðar Svavarsson spent a winter here 14 years before the first permanent settlers arrived.

Dominating the town above the harbour is the two-storey, cross-shaped timber church, built in 1907. **Safna-húsid**, the local museum (Stórigardur), has a natural history collection that includes a stuffed polar bear. It is said that drift ice brought the animal to the Icelandic coast from eastern Greenland during a severe winter.

On boat excursions from Húsavík and during the onward journey along Highway 85 around the Tjörnes peninsula, tourers will see just off the coast the island of **Lundey**, whose name means 'Puffin Island' and, of course, many of these birds nest here. Below you on the east side of the peninsula lies the broad **Öxarfjördur** inlet with the most striking sandur (spit formations) in northern Iceland. Jökulsá á Fjöllum, a huge glacial river originating on the northern edge of Vatnajökull, formed this part of Iceland over many thousands of years. Back in the mists of time, ★★ **Ásbyrgi** was a waterfall, but then a volcanic eruption or an earthquake changed the course of the river and a horseshoe-shaped gorge, opening out to the sea and closed off from the interior by rock faces up to 100m (330ft) high, was left behind.

The gorge of Ásbyrgi

★★ **Jökulsárgljúfur National Park**, of which Ásbyrgi is a part, is often described as Iceland's Grand Canyon. The park lines a most impressive river course some 25km (16 miles) long, up to 120m (400ft) deep and 500m (1,650ft) wide. At many points its walls are decorated with basalt columns or arches, interspersed with huge basalt sculptures, all shaped over thousands of years by the Jökulsá á Fjöllum river.

There is a series of spectacular waterfalls along the length of the canyon. From a viewpoint near Highway 864 it is possible to get a bird's eye view of **Hafragilsfoss**. A little further on a road leads up to ★★ **Dettifoss**, Europe's most prolific waterfall. The water of the Jökulsá, coloured grey by tons of sediment, cascades down 44m (150ft). A short walk upriver is **Selfoss waterfall**, not quite so spectacular, but still very photogenic. This alternative route rejoins the Ring Road near Grímsstadir.

Waterfall in the Jökulsárgljúfur

Welcoming sight in the wilderness

As the road heads eastward, the landscape becomes lonelier and increasingly barren. The farm at **Mödrudalur** (674km/418 miles) is the highest (470m/1,541ft) and one of the most remote in the country. When the tiny church appears out of the wilderness, it is a welcoming sight.

The next 45km (28 miles) passes through a desert of gravel and ash with almost no vegetation, a landscape very

A landscape of gravel and ash

similar to the central highlands. A gem in this desolate part of the country is the turf-covered ★ **Sænautasel** farmhouse (698km/433 miles), which was re-opened in 1994 after 50 years of gradual decay. Built in 1843, it has been lovingly restored and is now used as a café in summer.

As you walk to your coffee and cakes, you cross a stream via a bridge which is a small-scale but accurate reconstruction of an 18th-century bridge that crossed the Jökulsá á Brú river. This glacial river, which the road follows for many kilometres, sweeps up to 120 tonnes of sand and gravel per hour from a large area at the northeastern corner of Vatnajökull out to sea, thus creating one of Iceland's busiest conveyor belts. Near the school at **Brúarás**, used in the summer as inexpensive accommodation, plus cafeteria, the grey water squeezes through a deep and narrow canyon. At this point Iceland's highest bridge crosses the river. This one was built in 1994 to replace a dilapidated predecessor built in the 1930s. According to local legend, there was a natural bridge here which survived until the 16th century, when it collapsed. At the end of that century, Hanseatic merchants paid for Iceland's first man-made bridge to be built.

Smile from Egilsstaðir

At **Fellabær** (770km/478 miles) the **Lagarfljót**, as the outflow of Lögurinn is called, is crossed by a 300-m (1,000-ft) long wooden bridge. On the other side of the bank lies **Egilsstaðir** (775km/481 miles), the modern but faceless 'capital' of eastern Iceland and the final destination for this route. Just over 1,600 people now live in what is the most important town in this region.

Certainly more charming than the town itself is the surrounding area, above all **Lögurinn**, which is just under 40km (25 miles) long, up to 2km (1¼ miles) wide and in places 112m (370ft) deep. But is it a river or a lake? Its waters move slowly but steadily towards the sea, the milky grey colour revealing that it is meltwater from the northern edge of the Vatnajökull ice-cap. Many visitors scan the water in vain for the legendary giant worm, Lagarfljótsormur – according to descriptions, a close relative of Nessie, the Loch Ness monster.

Birdlife of Lögurinn

It is possible to make a full circuit of Lögurinn (about 90km/56 miles). Near **Hallormsstaður** you can enjoy the rare opportunity to take a forest walk. Iceland's largest woodland area is popular with the locals in summer.

At the southern end of the lake stands the church at **Valþjófsstaður** that possesses a copy of a medieval wooden door. The original, one of the most precious pieces of wood-carving in the country, is kept in the National Museum in Reykjavík. To the north at **Skriðuklaustur**, the former residence of the Icelandic writer Gunnar Gunnarsson (1889–1975) can be seen on the site of an his-

toric monastery. Gunnarsson's reputation is still disputed in Iceland, as he had sympathies with Nazi Germany, where he enjoyed his greatest literary successes – a fate which he shared with the Norwegian Nobel Prize winner, Knut Hamsun. It is said that the house that he built in 1939 was designed by Hitler's favourite architect, Höger.

Scenery near Seyðisfjörður and a local dwelling

A track that is only suitable for 4-wheel drive vehicles branches off to the permanently snow-covered **Snæfell** and to the northern edge of **Vatnajökull**, one of the toughest regions for hikers anywhere in Iceland.

A point a little further on from the bridge over the Hengifossá marks the start of a good 2-hour walk along the river to the basalt-columned ★ **Litlanesfoss** waterfall and its 120-m (393-ft) high counterpart, ★ **Hengifoss**. Return to Egilsstapir via Fellabær.

The harbour for the summer-only ferry that links Iceland with the rest of Europe is at **Seyðisfjörður**, one of Iceland's few truly attractive coastal towns. It is mainly the houses around the jetty, most of which date from the end of the 19th century, that lend the fishing village its charm. These dwellings recall the boom years when Norwegian fish merchants had bases here. Seyðisfjörður obtained its municipal charter in 1895. Since then its population has dwindled to just under 800.

As the ferry to the European mainland sets sail on Thursday (from mid-May to mid-September), many of the campsites and other forms of accommodation in the vicinity are full to capacity just prior to its departure. If you are not intending to catch the ferry, it is a good idea to steer clear of the Egilsstaðir/Seyðisfjörður region on Wednesday and Thursday. Whatever your plans, it is essential to book mid-week accommodation in advance.

If you are on your way home and in need of some mementoes or gifts, visit **Islandsouvenirs** at Norðurgata 8.

Exploring the Skálafellsjökull

Route 3

Along the Ring Road through Iceland's east and south

Egilsstaðir – Reyðarfjörður – Höfn – Vatnajökull – Kirkjubæjarklaustur – Vík – Reykjavík (750km/466 miles) *See map on page 26*

This route begins with a journey along the Eastfjords. Although the attractions of this landscape are obvious, they are still to be discovered by many visitors to Iceland. The road runs through an impressive fjord landscape beneath several striking mountain peaks. To the south of Djúpivogur it runs beside a series of lagoons. Narrow spits of gravel and sand deposited by the glacial rivers push out between the bays and the open sea.

Ice-cold encounter near the Vatnajökull

Höfn marks the start of the south coast. For the next 150km (93 miles) this route follows closely one of the most spectacular landscapes on earth: the Vatnajökull ice-cap with its many valley glaciers, drifting icebergs on the Jökulsárlón glacial lake and the dramatic Skaftafell National Park. The route also offers plenty of opportunities for detours. One option is a tour of the colourful rhyolite mountains of Landmannalaugar. Another possibility is a foray to the Þorsmörk valley, framed by glaciers and glacial rivers.

A bus service links Egilsstaðir, Höfn and Reykjavík. Public transport also covers all the detours described in this route. While the Ring Road follows the shorter route over the 470m (1,541ft) high Breiðdalsheiði to the Breiðdalur valley, Route 3 leaves Egilsstaðir *(see page 40)* to the southeast along good, mainly asphalt roads by the fjords. When the fjord road rejoins the Ring Road in Breiðdalsvík, you will have done an extra 45km (28 miles).

Do not expect to see anything spectacular by the Mjóifjörður inlet, but nature lovers will not want to miss it. The 600-m (1,975-ft) high, bare and inhospitable Mjóafjarðarheiði has to be climbed and there could be snow on the ground at almost any time in the year. The road then snakes its way down to the fjord passing waterfalls. A female troll, said to have once lived in the **Prestagil** ravine, would often lay in wait for priests, who made a tasty snack. More appetising, however, are the blueberries that grow at lower altitudes and can be picked in late August.

Waterfall at the Mjóijfördur inlet

Only about 30 people still live beside the fjord, most of them in **Brekka**. Situated here are the church, dating from 1892, and a school. In the summer the dormitories become the basic, but cosy Pension Sólbrekka (tel: 476 0007, cafeteria; $).

At the beginning of the 20th century, Mjóifjörður was one of the busiest settlements in eastern Iceland. Once 700 people lived here, staffing one of Iceland's first cold-storage warehouses. Some of the first telephones were installed here and for many years there was a small, private electricity generating station.

A track running tantalisingly close to the steep slopes that overlook the fjord goes as far as **Dalatangi**. At one time there were seven farmhouses here, now only one of them is inhabited. The lighthouse keeper's residence belongs to the nation. Beside the new lighthouse stands the ruin of Iceland's first coastal beacon.

43

Track to Dalatangi

The main route follows the coast. If you follow the suggested route you will reach the easternmost point of your round trip at **Vattarnes** lighthouse (64km/40 miles). Birding enthusiasts should continue for a few more kilometres and ask at the Vattnes farmhouse (tel: 475 1397) if there are likely to be any boat trips to the **Skrúður** bird rock, which lies offshore.

Fáskrúðsfjörður (81km/50 miles) has, like many fjord settlements, to cope with two names. The village is usually referred to by the name of the adjacent fjord, less often by its true place name, Búðir. Between 1880 and 1935 it was the base for a small French fishing colony. The many graves in the old cemetery at Fáskrúðsfjörður remind visitors of those times. Above the southern shores of the fjord towers the 743-m (2,437-ft) rhyolite Sandfell mountain.

Stöðvarfjörður (110km/68 miles) bears the alternative name of Kirkjuból. Just before leaving the village in the direction of Breiðdalsvík, you will pass the stone and mineral collection that Petra Sveinsdóttir has painstakingly assembled in her garden.

After a breathtaking stretch of road which crosses the steep Kambaskriður slopes high up above the coast, the route rejoins the Ring Road in **Breiðdalsvík** (130km/80

Lighthouse near Berunes

Austurhorn

miles) and then continues on towards Reykjavík. The road follows a southbound course along the shores of the Brei-ddalsvík inlet. At Berunes Youth Hostel (152km/94 miles), the village of Djúpivogur comes into view on the other side of the fjord.

Djúpivogur is less than 5km (3 miles) away, but the **Berufjörður** inlet sends motorists on a time-consuming detour. The coast road is some 40km (25 miles) long, but the superb mountain panorama of ridges and rugged peaks, in particular the 1,000-m (3,250-ft) high Búlandstindur pyramid above **Djúpivogur** (192km/119 miles), compensate for the extra distance. This village, the last place of any size before Höfn, a good 100km (60 miles) away by road, was a trading post for German merchants at the end of the 16th century.

The Ring Road runs around the edge of the settlement. Take a turning to the left to reach the centre of the village. The decent harbour here makes a good base for fishing and trade and provides a living for the 600 or so inhabitants. It is an important centre as, apart from Heimaey on the Westman Islands, there is only one other mainland harbour, the one at Höfn, between here and Þorlákshöfn, a short distance from Reykjavík.

To the southeast of Djúpivogur lies the tiny island of **Papey**, now home to thousands of sea birds. The name indicates that even before the first Norse settlers had arrived on Iceland, Celtic monks, known in the Viking language as '*papen*', lived here. For information about accommodation and organised tours to the island, call Papeyjarferdir on 478 8119.

The next inlet to the south, **Hamarsfjörður**, is a fjord in name, but this is where the straight coastline typical of the whole of southeast Iceland, begins. Where the fjord meets the sea, currents deposit banks of sand and gravel so that spits and lagoons form, making navigation in the inshore waters almost impossible.

By **Álftafjörður** and particularly the **Lón** lagoon, spit formation is well advanced. These are what geologists refer to as sandurs, flat expanses of outwash formed from sediment. Here it is the glacial rivers rising on Vatnajökull and several other smaller glaciers that have caused the build-up.

The **Austurhorn** (245km/152 miles), the northern limit of Lón, is a sugar loaf mountain formed from gabbro, a stone that is rare in Iceland. Unlike the surface rock which predominates elsewhere, gabbro is a deep-earth rock similar to granite.

The farmhouse at **Stafafell í Lón** (263km/163 miles) is a good base for those wishing to explore the impressive uplands at the eastern edge of Vatnajökull, the **Lónsöræfi** peaks – rugged and, in places, glaciated remnants of a central volcano dating from the tertiary era and an area for some demanding walks.

The **Almannaskarð** pass (282km/175 miles) is the steepest section of the Ring Road. Do stop and admire the magnificent view from the top. On a promontory, which separates the Hornafjörður and Skarpsfjörður lagoons, lies the town of Höfn. Two elongated spits close off the region from the sea. Further west lie seemingly endless sandurs, on top of which ice from Vatnajökull sparkles in the sun. If the weather is fine, try to arrange your day so that you can watch the sunset from the Almannaskarð pass – an incredible sight.

Höfn í Hornafirði (294km/182 miles) is a fishing village founded just under 100 years ago. In 1974 when the southern half of the Ring Road was completed and the land route to Reykjavík was no longer via Akureyri, the town enjoyed a boost to its prosperity. Höfn, with its 1,800 inhabitants, is now the largest town on the Ring Road between Akureyri and Selfoss, still a distance of more than 900km (560 miles).

A ★ **Seafarers and Fishermen's Memorial**, built in 1988, dominates the harbour area – the sea is the main source of employment for the inhabitants of Höfn. This memorial serves as a good viewpoint over the narrow passage between the two spits, which are gradually moving closer together. Fierce currents make the gap that lets boats pass out on to the open sea very dangerous, but it is the only way to reach the fishing grounds.

It is easy to return to the Ring Road from Höfn (298km/185 miles). At Smyrlabjörg hydro-electric power station (341km/211 miles), a ★ **mountain road**, only passable by conventional vehicles for the first few kilometres, forks off. Leave your car by the power station and travel by four-wheel drive bus (beginning of June to the beginning of September 1–2 times a day) along the spectacular track up to the Jöklasel mountain base on ★★ **Skálafellsjökull**.

Speeding on the Skálafellsjökull

At an altitude of 840m (2,756ft) on the edge of the ★★★ **Vatnajökull ice-cap** stands the Jöklasel restaurant, which boasts the best view in Iceland – one only bettered by views from the air. The vista to the south extends over Höfn, the flat inshore terrain and the Atlantic Ocean, while only a few metres away motor sleighs and snowmobiles stand ready to carry passengers away on an adventure over the eternal ice.

Travel on the Vatnajökull

If you do not wish to go up on to the glacier, then you can still experience the ice, as it extends down to the Ring Road. During the 19th century the **Breiðamerkurjökull** ice tongue (373km/231 miles) used to reach as far as the

Icy encounter on the Jökulsárlón

The Svartifoss

sea, but the glacier receded and the 150-m (492-ft) deep ★★ **Jökulsárlón** glacial lake and the 1.5-km (1-mile) long Jökulsá glacial river were formed. Floating on the lake against the spectacular backdrop of the huge ice-cap, broken up only by a few mountain peaks, are countless icebergs, their blue, white and black colour, dependent on air and ash content.

Boat trips out on to the world of ice are available throughout the summer months. There is a cafeteria beside the Jökulsárlón (beginning of June–end of August; tel: 478 1065; $).

Not quite so accessible to tourists, but then not quite so spectacular, is the **Breiðárlón** glacial lake (384km/238 miles) at the foot of **Fjallsjökull**. This glacial tongue is creeping down from **Öræfajökull**, the southernmost spur of the Vatnajökull ice-cap. Lying dormant underneath the ice is a volcano, which erupted in 1362 and then again in 1727, devastating the surrounding area on both occasions. **Hvannadalsshnúkur**, a peak that emerges from the Öræfajökull ice-cap, is Iceland's highest mountain (2,119m/6,952ft).

At its foot lies the settlement of **Fagurhólsmýri** (405km/251 miles), the centre of the Öræfi region. In the absence of a decent harbour and restricted by the vast glacial rivers to the east and west, the only route to the outside world for the people who lived here was for many centuries over the ice of Vatnajökull.

Try to make the worthwhile – and relatively inexpensive for Iceland – excursion by tractor and hay wagon (2–4 hours; tel: 478 1682) along a spit to the barrier island of **Ingólfshöfði**, where in 874 Ingólfur Arnarson, Iceland's first permanent settler, lived for some time before moving on to Reykjavík. Seals and sea birds are always visible, occasionally whales. Ingólfshöfði is a nature conservation area with the largest puffin colony on the south coast.

Hof (408km/253 miles) is a small settlement with a pretty turf-covered church dating from 1884.

It is not far to the entrance to the ★★ **Skaftafell National Park** (428km/265 miles). Framed by glaciers, this region of woodland and moor can boast several places of interest and ranks as one of Iceland's top sights. Allow at least two hours for a walk to the dramatic **Svartifoss** waterfall, which is backed by a wall of basalt columns.

If you wish to visit Iceland's only overhanging glacier, ★ **Morsárjökull**, set aside at least one day. Ice blocks often break off and crash over a mountain ledge into the valley. Alternatively, you may wish to see where the Skeiðará river emerges from the Skeiðarárjökull. In November 1996, vast quantities of water gushed out from under the glacier, melted by a sub-glacial volcano. A detailed brochure that shows all the footpaths in the vicinity is available from the information office at the national park's administrative centre.

Route 3 crosses **Skeiðarársandur**, Iceland's largest sandur, to the west of Skaftafell. In November 1996 about 8km (5 miles) of National Highway 1 were washed away in the *jökulhlaup* or glacier burst. It was at this point in 1974 that the highway became a ring road. The glacial rivers that cut across the sand and gravel flats were finally bridged. **Lómagnúpur**, the 777-m (2,549-m) high cape, marks the western end of Skeiðarársandur. Visible here are the land uplift and also the sand and gravel, which were deposited at the same time. In primordial times the sea crashed against Lómagnúpur's rocks. Situated at its foot now is the **Núpsstaður** farmstead (462km/287 miles) with its original stable buildings and turf-covered chapel dating from 1659. From here the coastline runs south for more than 20km (12 miles).

Núpsstaður farmstead

47

Kirkjubæjarklaustur (495km/307 miles) has only about 200 inhabitants, but the school and trading centre serve a wide catchment area. Irish monks lived here before the arrival of the Norse settlers. A Benedictine monastery survived from 1186 until the Reformation and many of the names for local geographical features refer to the convent's nuns. Examples include ★ **Systrastapi** ('Sisters' Rock'), ★ **Systrafoss** ('Sisters' Waterfall') and **Systravatn** ('Sisters' Lake'). Near Highway 203, which leads to the campsite, is **Kirkjugólf** ('Church Floor'), a smooth surface formed from natural basalt.

When the Laki crater erupted in 1783 *(see page 14)*, Kirkjubæjarklaustur would have been destroyed had the pastor not brought the wall of fire to a standstill by delivering a passionate sermon. Known as **Nýja-Eldhraun**

Systrafoss near Kirkjubæjarklaustur

Heading for the Laki crater

The Fjardará canyon

or 'Fire Lava', the resulting field of lava covers an area of 550 sq. km (212 sq. miles) and is the largest recorded lava flow from one eruption since the Settlement. The Ring Road crosses the expanse of lava to the west of Kirkjubæjarklaustur and is now overgrown with moss. Depending on how much rain has fallen, the block lava appears either as a rich green or a dull grey colour.

The track (501km/311 miles) that leads to the ★ **Laki crater** is only suitable for four-wheel drive vehicles or the special bus (July/August daily from Kirkjubæjarklaustur). **Fjardará canyon**, however, a spectacular gorge, can be reached in any vehicle (a further 5km/3 miles). The Fjardará river has carved its way through the earth and created a narrow but very deep and craggy canyon – in some places only a few metres wide.

The Ring Road now crosses the Kúdafljót glacial river via a new bridge (1994; older maps will not show the bridge – the original route means an extra 8km/5 miles). The kingdom of Vatnajökull now lies behind you; ahead are **Mýrdalsjökull** and the notorious **Mýrdalssandur**. After crossing this sand-and-gravel desert it used to be the custom to leave 'good-luck' cairns made from layers of stone by the roadside. Many modern-day tourists continue this tradition.

Mýrdalssandur's bad name stems from two phenomena. Fierce sandstorms can in extreme cases remove rust, even paint, from a car in much the same way that buildings are cleaned by sandblasting. Beside the road travellers can see how attempts have been made to stabilise the sand with vegetation. Vigilance and modern scientific methods give some warning about the second danger. Lying dormant beneath the ice of Mýrdalsjökull is the Katla volcano, which has boiled over 16 times since the settlement of Iceland, i.e. approximately every 70 years. The last eruption was in 1918, so the next one is now overdue. When the volcano becomes active beneath the ice, a devastating wall of water floods Mýrdalssandur. Two mountains tower above this plain. Undoubtedly both were originally islands, which as a result of land uplift and silting have lost contact with the sea.

Nearer to the coast lies **Hjörleifshöfdi** (554km/344 miles). According to the *Landnámabók (see page 13)*, Leifur, blood brother and companion of the first Icelander, Ingólfur Arnarson, lived here for some time before falling victim to a slave revolt.

Vík í Mýrdal (566km/352 miles) is a little town situated in a picturesque valley. It can offer travellers all the main amenities. Excursions on amphibious vehicles to some dramatic offshore rock formations are available from the Víkurskáli service area (tel: 487 1334). For jeep tours into the hinterland and to Hjörleifshöfði, call 487 1332.

Although a coastal town, Vík has no harbour because of silting. One of the destinations that can be reached from Vík is Iceland's southern cape, **Dyrhólaey**. There is a striking natural arch, topped by a photogenic lighthouse. Dyrhólaey or 'Door Hill Island' was originally an underwater volcano, but it grew into an island. Over many thousands of years part of it has merged with the Icelandic mainland. The coast is gradually shifting to the south, as new material from the glacial rivers is deposited on the shores and it is quite possible that in a few hundred years' time hikers will be able to pass through the arch carved by the Atlantic breakers.

Dyrhólaey

A track (581km/361 miles) runs from the Ring Road to the Dyrhólaey plateau. Although this involves an extra 5km (3 miles), it is well worth making the short journey for the magnificent view it affords of the coast.

By the **Sólheimajökull** glacier (access at 595km/370 miles) lies the centre of glacier tourism on Mýrdalsjökull. Available here are summer skiing and motorised sleigh excursions (Snjósleðaferðir, tel: 568 8888).

49

In **Skógar** (601km/373 miles) the 60-m (200-ft) high ★★ **Skógafoss** thunders over the cliffs of the old coastline. It is very rare to see such a powerful waterfall from this angle. You arrive at the falls at the lower end. It may be tempting to take a shower, but the weight of water would probably be fatal.

Skógafoss

Drive on instead to the thermal swimming pool at **Seljavellir** (turn off at 609km/378 miles). You can sit in a 'hot pot' here and enjoy the mountain panorama. ★ **Seljalandsfoss** (628km/390 miles) provides another encounter with water. It is possible here to follow the waterfall along a downhill path. Soon after you will cross the **Markarfljót** glacial river on a new bridge. This watercourse carries meltwater from the Eyjafjallajökull and Mýrdalsjökull glaciers down to the sea.

Some way inland in the rain shadow of Eyjafjallajökull is the peaceful woodland area of the ★★ **Þórsmörk Valley**. Surrounded by a rugged glacier backdrop, it is one of the most popular destinations on the highland fringes and has several mountain cabins and campsites.

Þórsmörk Valley

A variety of walking tours start here. One undemanding option is an afternoon walk through the nearby woods. For those seeking something a little more challenging, try a mountain walk southwards to the coast near Skógar. Dedicated trekkers might prefer to investigate a four-day hike to **Landmannalaugar**. Þórsmörk can be reached only in a large four-wheel-drive vehicle or as part of a bus trip from Hvolsvöllur (650km/404 miles; *see overleaf*).

Iceland's edible berries include black crowberries and blueberries

Hvolsvöllur marks the beginning of the more densely populated region of Iceland. Some of the farmhouse names have connections with the medieval sagas, in particular the Njálssaga.

Selfoss (700km/435 miles) has a population of about 4,300 and is the largest inland town in Iceland. It occupies an important position in the road network of southwest Iceland and is the centre of what is predominantly an agricultural region. The main employer in the town is one of northern Europe's largest dairies. A folk and natural history museum (June–August, daily 2–5pm) is situated in Tryggvagata.

The greenhouse town of **Hveragerði** (712km/442 miles) can demonstrate its unique expertise in using geothermal energy to overcome the harsh North Atlantic climate. Exotic flowers and Mediterranean fruit are grown here under glass. The cultivation of vegetables and pot plants is of commercial importance, too. Growers here largely meet the Icelanders' demand for tomatoes, cucumbers and peppers. Some of the greenhouses sell their products to the passing public at very reasonable prices. The hot water that flows from the underground springs is, of course, the source of energy.

Practically every coach party stops at **Eden**, Austurmörk 25, tel: 483 4900. The attractions here are the greenhouse, a huge souvenir shop with the largest collection of postcards on Iceland and a café that serves rather pricey snacks under palm trees.

The Ring Road gradually snakes its way up to **Hellisheiði** and, after crossing a 1,000-year-old lava plateau, finally reaches ★ **Reykjavík** (750km/466 miles).

Detour to the Westman Islands

The Westman archipelago, which consists of 15 islands and about 30 skerries and rocks, was formed during the past 10,000 to 20,000 years on what is one of the most volcanically active belts in the world. It was basically a case of one eruption equals one island. Only one exception, the inhabited **Heimaey** island, was formed from a series of eruptions.

Heimaey Island and some of the damage in 1973

On 23 January 1973, without any warning, a new volcano, later to be christened Eldfell or 'Fire Mountain', erupted on the eastern side of the Heimaey town. Lava and ash buried 400 houses for ever, but the 6,000 inhabitants of Heimaey came to no harm as they were all evacuated during the night. Because there had been a storm the day before, the island's fishing fleet was at anchor in harbour and fortuitously the crews were on hand to rescue all the islanders from the fiery explosion.

This eruption lasted for about six months, during which time volunteers tried to protect house contents from the

*Countless puffins
nest on Heimaey*

lava and the constant showers of ash. At one point a lava
flow threatened to destroy the town's natural harbour, an
important part of the fishing community's livelihood. In
desperation, helpers showered millions and millions of
litres of seawater over the advancing river of molten lava
and, despite all predictions to the contrary, they managed
to bring the flow to a standstill and, remarkably, in such
a way that the harbour entrance is now better protected
than it was before.

51

The 5,000 inhabitants of the Heimaey fishing community make up less than two percent of the Icelandic population, yet they account for some 15 percent of their
country's exports.

The residents of Heimaey now live only a few metres
from the wall of lava. This tourist attraction is best viewed
from Kirkjuvegur and Heimagata.

On the island's shores the sea has created steep cliffs
and spectacular caves. Millions of sea birds nest here,
including countless puffins. These birds form part of the
Westman Islanders' diet, along with guillemots, the eggs
of the stormy petrel and also sea grass, which is collected
on the coast.

Offspring on their way

Heimaey's Natural History Museum (open 1 May–
1 September, daily 11am–5pm, otherwise only Saturday
and Sunday 3–5pm) has an interesting display of stuffed
birds, with the emphasis mainly on those species that
nest on the island. Tanks keep samples of the fish that
are caught around the islands.

In September 1998 the island welcomed a new guest:
Keiko, the killer whale and star of the film *Free Willy*, was
for many years a prisoner in an American oceanarium. The
mammal was brought here to prepare it for a life of free-
dom in the North Atlantic. Just how long it will remain
in its present enclosure in a bay by the entrance to Heimaey
harbour, nobody is quite sure.

Natural History Museum

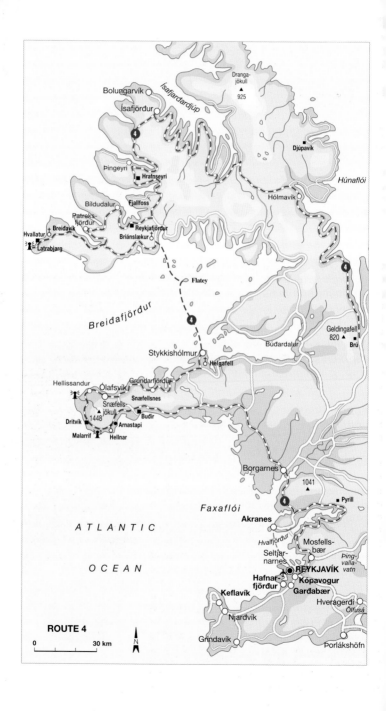

ROUTE 4

0 _____ 30 km

N

Route 4

Circular tour via Snæfellsnes and through the Westfjords

Reykjavík – Snæfellsjökull – Stykkishólmur – Flatey – Látrabjarg – Ísafjörður – Brú (1,031km/640 miles)

This route goes round the tip of the Snæfellsnes peninsula, where you will see one of the finest mountains in the world, the ice-capped Snæfellsjökull volcano which, at 1,446 metres (4,743 ft), dominates the countryside. From Stykkishólmur, an attractive little town, the ferry sails through the Breiðafjörður islands to the largely unexplored Westfjords. While very popular with bird enthusiasts, the region is also essential viewing for lovers of remote, spectacular landscapes.

Out of the land mass – one of the oldest in Iceland – natural forces have forged a series of fjords – fingers of water that cut deep into the peninsula. Beyond the narrow, thinly populated coastal strip, steep slopes ascend to lonely mountain ridges and marshy plateaux. Impressive cliffs, long stretches of sandy beaches, magnificent waterfalls, a few hot springs and one glacier reveal the full splendour of the diverse landscape so typical of Iceland.

Travelling in the northwest requires more time than other regions, partly because the weather can be very unpredictable. You should allow three days for this route – although there are easily enough sights to keep most travellers occupied for a week. The section around Snæfellsjökull can be covered in a day, albeit a strenuous one, from Reykjavík.

Dramatic coast near Arnastapi

53

Exploring the terrain

Leave **Reykjavík** *(see page 18)* on the northern Ring Road. The Hvalfjörður tunnel (toll: ISK 1,000), opened in 1998, saves about 50km (31 miles) or about an hour of driving along winding roads beside the fjord. It is, nevertheless, worth the effort if the weather is fine *(see page 28)*. All distances for Route 4 include the detour around the fjord.

Borgarnes (pop. 1,800; 117km/73 miles) is one of the most important towns in western Iceland and a hub for traffic on the Snæfellsnes peninsula and the Westfjords. It occupies a special place among Iceland's towns – it is situated beside the sea but, unusually, fishing plays no part in the local economy.

The town's attraction for tourists lies in its association with figures from the Icelandic sagas, in particular the famous *Egils Saga*. Skallagrímur Kveldúlfsson, the first settler in the region and father of the saga hero, Egill Skallagrímsson, is said to be buried in a small park in the

town centre, together with Bödvar, his grandson. Just north
of the town, where Highway 54 branches off the Ring Road
towards Snæfellsnes, lies **Borg á Myrum** farmhouse
where the two lived during the 10th century. Some 200
years later, Egill's descendant, the diplomat and scholar
Snorri Sturluson, assumed to be the writer of the *Egils
Saga*, married into the Borg family.

The **Snæfellsnes** peninsula is not one of Iceland's most
active volcanic zones, but the first summit you will see
(152km/94 miles) is the **Eldborg** volcano or 'Fire Fort'.
This very evenly formed crater rises about 60m (200ft)

Basalt columns on Snæfellsnes

from a field of lava. Huge basalt columns on the **Gerðu-
berg** (164km/102 miles), visible from the road to the Höfði
farmhouse, are reminders of earlier volcanic activity. If
you follow this road northwards for 5.5km (just under
3½ miles) as far as an overgrown lava field, you will
discover **Rauðamelsökelda** spring (10 minutes' walk).
The carbonated flow tastes much better than any bottled
mineral water.

Water from a warm spring is used for the hot pots at
the swimming pool in **Lýsuhóll** school and community
centre (212km/132 miles).

On a clear day, the ice-capped ★★ **Snæfellsjökull** volcano,
with two other summits close by (1,442m/4,730ft and
1,446m/4,744ft), will quickly come to dominate the sky-
line. Jules Verne took Snæfellsjökull as the starting point
for the heroic adventures he described in *Journey to the
Centre of the Earth,* and Iceland's Nobel prize winner
for literature, Halldór Laxness *(see page 73),* chose to
use the volcano as the backdrop for his novel *Under the
Glacier,* an acerbic attack on the church.

Route 4 now follows coastal highway 574 around

Snæfellsjökull

Snæfellsjökull. The traditional **Hótel Búðir** *(see page 80)*

s situated in a picturesque spot on the edge of an ancient, vergrown lava field. Only a few metres away, past an ttractive timber church and a small cemetery, lies an dyllic beach, where the sand dunes contrast strikingly vith the pitch black lava rock. When the weather is fine, he snow-covered Snæfellsjökull glacier makes an attrac- ive backdrop.

Approach Snæfellsjökull passing large farmhouses dot- ed along the flat strip of land between the mountain slopes ind the shoreline. A four-wheel-drive vehicle is needed to ipproach the volcano's east flank via track F570, but it s possible to take an ordinary car the few hundred metres o **Sönghellir** echo cave, the starting point for some fine glacier walks. It should be pointed out, however, that a guide with experience of glaciers is essential and all the necessary safety measures must be taken. Some fatal acci- dents have occurred on Snæfellsjökull, because the dan- gers have been underestimated. Guided tours on the glacier ire organised from the Hótel Búðir, from Arnastapi and from Ólafsvík *(see page 56)*.

The church at Búðir

Arnastapi (238km/148 miles) is the tourist gateway to Snæfellsjökull, and is also famous for its birdlife and its spectacular coastline formations of basalt caves and bridges. The distinctive symbol for this settlement is the huge stone monument to Bárður Snæfellsás, a character from the medieval sagas.

Basalt bridge at Arnastapi

The basalt coast is just as impressive by the next vil- age, **Hellnar**, some 2km (1¼ miles) from the main road. Make a point of exploring the sea-level *Baðstofa* or 'Bath- room' cave, where bizarre effects of light and colour can be seen. The rocks beside the two rock pillars of **Lón- drangar** (246km/152 miles) are among the best vantage points in the whole of Iceland for observing sea birds.

Monument to Bárður Snæfellsás

Snæfellsjökull shows its best face over the next few kilometres, particularly on summer evenings. Solidified lava flows formed many thousands of years ago can fire the imagination. The volcano beneath the glacier cap has never erupted during the human history of Iceland, but it is not considered extinct.

After 250km (155 miles) a road branches off to the sea. It is a half-hour walk from the end to the former fishing village of **Dritvík**. Abandoned many years ago, there is now nothing left but wilderness, although it is still pos- sible to pick out some foundation walls. If the spectacu- lar lava coast is bathed in the golden evening sunlight, then the atmosphere is idyllic; when the harsh west wind blows, however, this is a raw and inhospitable place.

The road steers a course between glacier and sea through fields of lava of varying ages. Smallish craters can be spotted from time to time. The first sign of habitation is the tallest structure in Iceland, the 412-m (1,351-ft) high transmitter mast at **Gufuskálar** (275km/171 miles). A little further on, on the edge of **Hellissandur** (278km/173 miles), is a small folk museum that charts the history of fishing and seafaring in the region.

When fishermen had only small flat-bottomed rowing boats and an auxiliary sail, it was important that the men lived near their fishing grounds. There was no need for a harbour. All they required was a sandy beach.

During the season several hundred fishermen lived in places like Dritvík. Even though they fished the nearby waters, the work was very demanding. Before throwing out their nets the men often had to row hard for four to five hours and a fishing expedition could take up a whole day. If the catches were good, the men would go out to sea again, sometimes making two, three, even four trips one after the other.

Only fit men could do this work. What separated the men from the boys were the lifting stones that can still be seen in Djúpalón bay near Dritvík and in other places. To secure a place on one of the fishing boats, a man had to lift the 50kg (100lb) *hálfdrættinger* stone. Professional fishermen could lift the 140kg (300lb) *hálfsterkur* and many even managed to lift the 155kg (350lb) *fullsterkur* a metre above the ground.

Commercial fishing started in Iceland in the 16th century. The abandoned settlements now seen on the west coast of Snæfellsnes enjoyed their best years during the 17th and 18th centuries. With the arrival of enclosed sailing boats in the mid-19th century, followed by the steam-driven trawlers from 1906 onwards, deepwater harbours were necessary and at that time there were none in this part of Iceland. The fishermen who had once earned a good living on the peninsula were forced to move away.

Fisherman sculpture at Hellissandur

Church in Hellissandur

The harbour in **Ólafsvík** keeps many of the 1,200-plus inhabitants in work (288km/179 miles), but proximity to Snæfellsjökull also boosts income from tourism. A modern church and a warehouse dating from the middle of the 19th century, now home to the tourist information office, are worth investigating.

The modern church in Ólafsvík

A well-equipped, deep-sea catamaran, *Brimún*, based in Ólafsvík, is used for observing whales off the Snæfellsnes peninsula (June–August once daily, up to 7 hours; about £40). The huge mammals, mainly blue whales up to 190 tonnes in weight and 34m (110ft) long, are sighted on over 90 percent of trips. There are thought to be between 5,000 and 15,000 such creatures worldwide, about 1,000 of them in the North Atlantic around Iceland.

Route 4 follows Highway 57 eastwards along the north coast of the Snæfellsnes peninsula. The pyramid-shaped **Kirkjufell** (463m/1,520ft) near **Grundarfjörður** (316km/ 196 miles) is one of the most beautiful and most striking mountains in Iceland. The road hugs the coastline for a while and then follows a new course past the legendary **Berserkjahraun**, a lava field at least 4,000 years old. In the Saga Age 'berserks' were wild and burly warriors who sought to boost their strength in battle by wearing animal furs. The Berserkjahraun is named after two such fighting men. According to the Eyrbyggjasaga, a farmer enlisted the two men to clear a path through the lava to his brother's farm, but instead of paying them, the farmer killed them. They were apparently buried in a deep pit in the Berserkjahraun beside the path that they had hewn.

The destination for the path was **Bjarnarhöfn** farm by the coast. The present owner uses it as a base for shark fishing. Visitors to the farm can observe the traditional methods of shark processing and even sample some of the meat (tel: 438 1581).

At the foot of the colourful rhyolite **Drápuhlíðarfjall** peak (353km/219 miles), the result of volcanic activity, a road forks off to the left to Stykkishólmur. This passes the sacred **Mount Helgafell** (73m/240ft), a shrine in pagan times, later the site of an Augustinian monastery.

The futuristic **church** in one of Iceland's most delightful towns (363km/226 miles) dominates the area. Strangely, the bell-tower, now a symbol for ★ **Stykkishólmur**, is structurally too weak for any bells. Was this an attempt by government-inspired Protestants to break the dominance of the Dutch-run Catholic convent? The monastery complex, built in 1936 and also home to the regional hospital, dominates the port area. There are some stunning views from the island of **Súgandisey** – accessible via a causeway from the harbour – over the 3,000-

57

Stykkishólmur

plus islands, islets and rocks in Breiðafjörður and also over the mountain panorama behind Stykkishólmur. It is definitely worth making the short walk – on light summer evenings this is a truly romantic spot.

Many of the older buildings in the harbour area have been preserved. The **Norwegian House**, for example, imported in kit form from Norway and built in 1828, was the first two-storey private dwelling on Iceland. It is now home to the **Byggðasafn Snæfellinga og Hnappdœla** regional museum (Skólastígur 1; summer months 11am–5pm). The library makes a good vantage point for views over the town centre and harbour.

The journey by ferry through the labyrinth of islands in ★ **Breiðafjörður** is one of the highlights of this tour of western Iceland. The *Baldur* makes one or two sailings per day, depending on the time of year, from Stykkishólmur to Brjánslækur. The boat stops off at the island of ★ **Flatey**, the site of a 12th-century monastery and a major cultural centre until the 1800s. If the weather is fine, then it is a good idea to catch the morning ferry and stop over until the afternoon ferry arrives. As Flatey is a motor vehicle-free zone, you will have to leave your vehicle on the ferry anyway. It is then driven on to land by the crew in Brjánslækur and can be collected later.

A tour of the island village is like a journey back in time. Barely a handful of people live here all year round. Only during the summer months does the population grow to several hundred. Former islanders or their families often return to their roots at holiday time.

The bird life on Flatey and the surrounding skerries is a source of fascination for both ornithologists and laymen. Excursions for short-stay visitors can be booked on the *Baldur*. If you are intending to stay longer on the island, check carefully about the availability of provisions.

Gulls on Flatey

A stern stone figure guards the route west to Patreksfjörður

From the landing stage at **Brjánslækur** (campsite nearby), this route will take you to the westernmost point in Europe. First you must cross the 400-m (1,300-ft) high **Kleifaheiði** to reach **Patreksfjörður**. Be prepared for a fright if you are travelling in the mist. A stone figure with a stern expression looks down on travellers from the roadside. Road builders erected this monument in memory of their predecessors.

At the end of Patreksfjörður (405km/252 miles), Highway 612 branches off to Látrabjarg. As a symbol of progress, Iceland's first steel trawler stands in a field by the roadside.

The ★ **Minjasafn Egils Ólafssonar** museum in **Hnjótur** farmstead (429km/267 miles) is packed full of exhibits documenting the history of agriculture, fishing, seafaring and aviation in the region. The collection was the brainchild of a farmer whose name it bears. In front of the building stands a replica of a Viking ship and a Russian aeroplane.

Breiðavík, once a busy fishing harbour *(see page 56)* consists of a small church and what used to be a boarding school. It is worth taking a stroll along the magnificent sandy beach – Breiðavík means 'broad bay'.

The neighbouring village of **Hvallátur** also used to be a thriving fishing port. Look for the heavy lifting stones by the shore. Recruits for fishing expeditions would have been asked to lift them by their masters as a test of strength *(see page 56)*.

A narrow road runs from here to the westernmost point in Europe, **Cape Bjargtangar**, one of the ★★ **Látrabjarg** cliffs (455km/283 miles). Countless sea birds nest on these 14-km (9-miles) long and up to 444-m (1,456-m) high, often vertical, basalt rocks, probably the most dramatic section of the Icelandic coastline.

Birdwatching at Látrabjarg

Puffins can often be seen in the car-park only a few metres from the lighthouse; these attractive creatures are very happy to be photographed. If you take a walk along the cliff top, you can watch fulmars dancing above the precipice. Perched on the ledges lower down are guillemots and razorbills – the world's largest population of this species make their home on this headland. Look down over the rock face and you will see the shags watching the shoreline from the front row.

You must now retrace your steps along Highway 62 (505km/313 miles). Under a local government reorganisation scheme, the port of **Patreksfjörður** (517km/321 miles) has merged with the neighbouring settlements as far as Bildudalur (545km/339 miles) to create the com-

Braced against the elements

munity of **Vesturbyggð**. The northern section of this municipality lies beside one of the arms of the vast **Arnarfjörður**, the 'Eagle Fjord'.

Reykjafjörður (563km/350 miles) or 'Smoky Fjord' means hot springs. It is well worth relaxing for a while in the warm roadside pool to summon up some strength for the arduous journey ahead. Up in the mountains you will join Highway 60 (580km/360 miles), which starts at the ferry terminal in Brjánslækur *(see page 58)*, from here only 14km (9 miles) away; the circuit via Látrabjarg involves a detour of 217km (134 miles).

On the bleak and remote Dynjandisheiði moor, the road reaches an altitude of 500m (1,600ft) before winding its way down to **Dynjandisvogur** bay.

Dynjandi waterfall

After 602km (374 miles) it is worth pulling up to admire one of Iceland's finest waterfalls, ★ **Dynjandi**, also known as Fjallfoss, which is situated a few hundred metres from the road. The water tumbles across a broad face down almost 100m (330ft) over curving basalt steps.

Just before the road turns away from the coast towards the next climb, you will pass the **Hrafnseyri** vicarage (622km/386 miles). It has been in existence since Viking times and was the birthplace of one of Iceland's most celebrated figures, Jón Sigurðsson. The museum and memorial recall the life of this tireless fighter for Icelandic independence.

The 300 inhabitants of **Þingeyri** (640km/398 miles) live mainly from fishing, but the village used to be a trading post and Hanseatic merchants were once active here. Continue along this road and you will come to one of Iceland's most important road-building projects. A three-way tunnel, almost 9km (5 miles) in length, connects Flateyri and Suðureyri with the Westfjords capital of Ísafjörður. Mountain bikers and walkers may prefer to take

Iceland's rugged western coast almost reaches the Arctic Circle

the old route over the mountains, if they wish to avoid the exhaust gases in the tunnel. If the weather is fine, they will be rewarded with some stunning views.

The area's only town of any significant size, Ísafjörður (690km/429 miles) can trace its history back to Iceland's Settlement. It was on this peninsula, where the old town centre is located, that the first settler, Helgi Hrólfsson, took land, naming the fjord where he built his farmhouse **Skutulsfjörður** or 'Harpoon Fjord', because he found an old harpoon on the beach.

Ísafjörður has been the main trading centre for the region since the late Middle Ages, initially under the control of Hanseatic traders, later under the Danish Trade Monopoly. In 1786 Ísafjörður obtained the status of an official trading post, one of only six in the country. At the end of the 19th century, the largest private trading company in Iceland at that time was based here, but during the 1920s it was taken over by a co-operative.

Ísafjörður local

61

A cluster of houses on the southern side of the Eyri peninsula date from the 18th century, when the Danes held sway. ★ **Byggðasafn Vestfjarða** is an interesting museum dedicated to maritime travel, trade and fishing (Suðurtangi; June–mid-September, daily 1–5pm)

Ísafjörður outgrew the Eyri peninsula a long time ago and now extends along the northwest shores of Skutulsfjörður. The town's leisure area is situated to the northwest in the valleys that run into the end of the fjord. There are many summer homes, a campsite in **Tungudal** and a winter sports centre in **Seljalandsdal**. Every year over the Easter week a skiing and folk festival is held in the town. The island of ★ **Vigur** is a popular destination for boat trips. The principal points of interest there are the bird life and a primitive farmhouse with Iceland's only surviving windmill.

The town itself provides a good vantage point for views over the mouth of the Ísafjarðardjúp fjord. There is also an interesting folk museum with a replica of the Ósvör fishing base, which dates from the time when fishermen used rowing boats. **Gullauga Goldsmiths**, at Hafnarstræti 4, sell gold and stone pieces at designer prices. If you are interested in buying locally produced handicrafts directly from the makers, take the trip to **Bolungarvík** (Drymla, Skólastigur 3–5), 15km (9 miles) to the north. Enquire at the tourist information office for opening times.

Plantlife

You will be able to enjoy the full splendour of the fjords as you continue southwards beside **Ísafjarðardjúp**. As the crow flies, it is only 40km (25 miles) to the end of the fjord system; but by road the journey is 175km (108 miles). The only major settlement on this section is

62

Súðavík. The centre of the village (pop. 200) was devastated by an avalanche during snowstorms in 1995 *(see page 15)*. At the end of the southernmost finger of land jutting out into this fjord system lies **Reykjanes** or 'Smoky Peninsula' (17km/10 miles from the main road). The thermal spring water is used for a swimming pool and sauna at a former school complex, now converted into a hotel and a restaurant, which stays open all year.

After the journey around Ísafjördur, Highway 61 crosses the **Steingrímsfjardarheidi** plateau, an almost Arctic moraine landscape. Until well into the first half of the 19th century, ice from the Drangajökull glacier, now retreated northwards, covered this inhospitable terrain.

By **Steingrímsfjördur**, Highway 643 branches off Route 4 to the sparsely populated and desolate **Strandir coast** in the north, a 102-km (63-mile) long cul-de-sac that reaches into an area which sees very little in the way of tourism. The journey is a veritable feast for the eyes. Seals can often be seen basking by the shore.

It would be wrong to expect a great deal of hospitality in **Djúpavík**, now more or less a ghost town, which until well into the 20th century prospered from the thriving fishing industry. When the herring shoals stayed away, it started to decay rapidly, so it is something of a surprise to find accommodation in the **Hótel Djúpavík**, an old fish processing factory *(see page 103)*.

At the end of the road travellers can recover from their exertions in one of Iceland's most primitive swimming pools. Only a stone's throw from the icy North Atlantic, the **Krossneslaug** is supplied by the pleasantly warm water that flows from a hot spring.

Hólmavík (pop. 450) is the only town of any size on the Strandir coast. Amenities for tourists include an information office (in summer, tel: 451 3465) where local handicrafts are sold. There is also a petrol station with a cafeteria and supermarket next door.

The route now runs southwards past **Húnaflói** bay and its continuation **Hrútafjördur**. You will see an increasing number of farmhouses, even the occasional photogenic church, with **Prestbakki** (1,005km/624 miles) probably making the most attractive snap for the photo album. On those stretches where the road runs alongside the shore, it will become apparent that the local farmers run a profitable sideline processing driftwood. Arctic sea currents from Siberia deliver large consignments of tree trunks free of charge.

Near **Brú** (1,031km/640 miles) the route finally meets up with the Ring Road again. It is 202km (125 miles) to Reykjavík, 230km (143 miles) to Akureyri.

Route 5

Gullfoss

Iceland for beginners and short-stay visitors

**Reykjavík – Gullfoss – Stóri-Geysir – Þingvellir –
Reykjavík (250km/155 miles)** *See map on page 64*

This route is the classic tour for new arrivals. It takes in
the greenhouse capital of Hveragerði, the Kerið explosion
crater, Gullfoss 'Golden Waterfall' and the hot springs
in Haukadalur with the active Strokkur geyser. There is
nowhere better to get a feel for Iceland's history than
Þingvellir National Park, where the Icelandic parliament,
the Althing, first assembled over 1,000 years ago. The
route can be completed within one day. Without the detour
to Stöng, it will take between eight and nine hours, otherwise allow 10 to 12 hours.

Haukadalur hot springs

Set out from **Reykjavík** *(see page 18)* along the southbound Ring Road. Bláfjöll to the south of the Ring Road
and Hengill to the north both provide good skiing with
downhills and cross-country tracks. The best time for skiing is during the months of February and March.

When you reach the eastern end of the barren **Hellisheiði** plain, the view over Iceland's southern coast opens
up and, on a clear day, it is possible to see as far as the
Westman Islands. Down below is the greenhouse town
of **Hveragerði** (38km/24 miles; *see Route 3 page 50)*.

Just before Selfoss you leave the Ring Road and follow
Highway 35 towards Gullfoss and Geysir.

The explosion crater of ★ **Kerið** (61km/38 miles) is a
fine example of what geologists call a maar, i.e. a shallow,
flat-floored crater probably formed by multiple explosive
eruptions. This one – the finest of its kind in Iceland – is
some 55m (180ft) deep and shaped like an amphitheatre.

Skálholt (85km/53 miles) was for a long time the spiritual capital of Iceland. From 1056 until the Reformation, which reached southern Iceland in 1541, it was the seat of 32 Catholic bishops. A counter-Reformation movement ended in 1550 with the beheading of the last Catholic bishop of northern Iceland, Jón Arason *(see page 31)*. A memorial stone here recalls this event.

Skálholt saw a further 13 Protestant bishops before an earthquake badly damaged the cathedral and the theological school, forcing the church dignitaries to move to Reykjavík. The present church (1956–63) is the eleventh to be built here. All its predecessors were of timber.

Þjórsárdalur

Soon after you reach Highway 30, Highway 32 forks off to **Þjórsárdalur**. This road, most of which is asphalted, offers stunning views over the Þjórsá river and towards one of the best-known and most active central volcanoes in Iceland, the 1,491-m (4,891-ft) high ★ **Hekla**. The last eruption from its 5-km (3-mile) long volcanic fissure occurred in 2000 and further eruptions could take place at any time. Many earlier visitors from the European mainland described Hekla as the 'gateway to hell', from where the cries of sinners could be heard. Instead of burning in hell, why not unwind in the warm water of the nearby **Þjórsárdalslaug** thermal bath (turn off after 30km/19 miles) while enjoying the magnificent mountain panorama.

Hekla

To reach ★ **Hjálparfoss** falls, which are decorated with basalt columns and split in two by a rock, take the short track that branches off near the bridge over the Fossá river (the turning is 30km/19 miles from Highway 32, open only in summer) and then follow the west bank of the river southwards for a few hundred metres.

Þjóðveldisbærinn, a reconstruction of a Viking house, was built in 1974 to mark the 1,100th anniversary of the

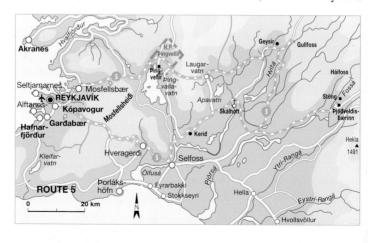

Settlement. The main room with a central fireplace was used as a workroom and communal dormitory. Only the farm owner and his wife enjoyed some privacy in the alcove along one side. Two annexes, each with one room, led off the main hall. One was the 'best room' where the women would sit spinning and weaving and where celebrations were held, the other was for the dairy cows and the preparation and storage of butter and milk. Do not be surprised by the size of the toilet opposite the entrance. During the Viking period 'spending a penny' was a collective activity.

Viking house entrance

Just before you reach the reconstruction, a rough track runs up to the north to the original building. **Stöng** farmhouse was buried under ash after Hekla erupted in 1104. Archaeologists uncovered the site in 1939, with medieval saga texts assisting in the excavation work. At the time of the volcanic eruption there were 15 farmhouses in this part of Þjórsárdalur. It is well worth taking the 30-minute walk from Stöng to see the **Gjáin** gorge and the splendid **Gjárfoss** waterfall.

The road continues northward via **Flúðir** (110km/68 miles) to ★★ **Gullfoss waterfall** (140km/87 miles). Here the Hvítá river, whose waters originate on the Langjökull glacier, drops a total of 32m (104ft) in two stages, deep into the **Gullfossgljúfur** gorge. On sunny afternoons it becomes clear why it is sometimes called the 'Golden Waterfall'. A monument recalls the courageous Sigríður Tómasdóttir (1871–1957), the daughter of a farmer from neighbouring Brattholt. She prevented the authorities from building a hydro-electric power station here, even though a British company had already signed the initial contract.

Gullfoss in winter

The geothermal region in the **Haukadalur** (146km/90 miles) is often described by its best-known spouting spring, the ★★ **Stóri-Geysir** ('Great Geyser'). For years this geyser was inactive and attempts were made to bring it back to life by pouring soap flakes down the tube. This, however, was deemed to be environmentally unacceptable, and in the end nature took its own course: in 2000 an earthquake awoke Great Geyser from its slumber and now once again columns of hot water shoot 60m (200ft) into the air. Its neighbour, ★★ **Strokkur**, reaches only about a third of this height, but can be relied upon to eject a jet of boiling hot water every few minutes.

Strokkur

Some of the other spouts around the site can discharge columns of very hot water, so it is important to watch where you walk and to read the notice boards.

In **Laugarvatn** ('Hot Spring Lake'; 180km/112 miles) a popular sauna draws its energy from the hot springs by the lake of the same name. There are several boarding schools in the village that become hotels in summer.

Þingvellir

Almannagjá gorge

Þingvallavatn is the second-largest lake in Iceland (exceeded in size only recently by the Þórisvatn reservoir; *see page 69*). ★★ **Þingvellir** (205km/127 miles) on its western shores, lies at the heart of a 50-sq.km (19-sq.mile) national park, opened in 1928. In 930 all the free men on the island met here for the first sitting of the Althing, the same Icelandic parliament that assembles in Reykjavík today. The site, of great importance to Icelanders, has no surviving buildings to admire, just some foundations to remind visitors of the búðir ('booths'), the shelters and meeting places where representatives conducted business.

A rock served as the official podium during parliamentary sessions. Every year in front of the assembly the parliament's speaker read out the law of the land, a wall of rock providing an acoustic aid. The **Öxará** river was diverted to improve the water supply. It now pours over into the ★ **Almannagjá** gorge *(see page 6 and below)* and flows right past the old parliament site. When the assembly was in session – usually once a year for 14 days – the legislators lived in tents and small huts.

A permanent assembly room was not built until the 17th century. To make up for the absence of any historical buildings, a **church** was constructed in 1859 and then, in two stages during the 20th century (1930 and 1974), the five-gabled **Þingvallabœr** was added. This is used by the national park rangers and church pastors. It is also available as a summer residence for Iceland's prime minister.

Þingvellir links together all the important dates in Icelandic history. With the introduction of Christianity in the year 1000, the old gods were given a good send-off here. In 1262 Icelanders gathered at the site and declared their loyalty to the Norwegian crown. Until the end of the 18th century, Þingvellir was the venue for the Lögrétta legislative committee, the last bulwark of the parliamentary system under an autocratic monarchy. Even though the Althing and the Lögrétta had moved to Reykjavík many years before, in 1874 the Icelanders adopted a new constitution here, formally removing power from the Danish crown. At the same time the nation celebrated its first 1,000 years. The new republic was proclaimed here in 1944 and in 1994 Iceland's 50th anniversary as an independent nation was marked by great celebrations.

From the north shore of Þingvallavatn a field of lava, restricted by two rifts, stretches deep inland: ★ **Almannagjá**, beside the old assembly in the west, and the less dramatic **Hrafnagjá** in the east. The Almannagjá or 'Everyman's Gorge' is 7km (4 miles) long and in some places it was wide enough to accommodate all the free men in the first Icelandic republic.

At **Mosfell** (240km/149 miles) you join the northbound Ring Road. It is now 10km (7 miles) back to **Reykjavík**.

Route 6

Hveravellir

Crossing the central highlands where the earth is barren and empty

The Kjölur Route (F35): Gullfoss – Hveravellir – Blöndudalur (180km/111 miles)
The Sprengisandur Route (F26): Sigalda – Sprengisandur – Goðafoss (234km/145 miles)
See map on page 26

67

Central Iceland offers a taste of adventure. It is a bleak and barren landscape like no other in Europe. Some of the smaller rivers have to be forded and tracks are often barely identifiable as they pass through seemingly endless fields of loose gravel. The appeal of the Icelandic highlands lies in its boundless dimensions. Glaciers and mountains on the horizon provide constant visual delights.

Both of these highland tracks can be covered in one day, but it is better to arrange accommodation, perhaps in the hiking clubs' mountain cabins.

The highland tracks are open to traffic only when they have firmed up after the snow has melted in late spring. If you intend to cross the highland plain in your own vehicle or by bus, do not arrive before the middle of July as the tracks may not be open. The dates given here are based on average values. More details are available from the website: www.vegag.is.

Scheduled buses run cross-country between Reykjavík and Akureyri and between Reykjavík and Mývatn.

Cauldron at Kjölur

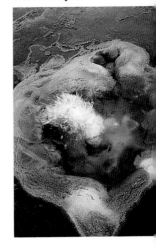

The Kjölur Route

The Kjölur Route, often closed by snow and ice until well into the summer, is an ancient track, which was used during the Middle Ages for driving cattle as it passes

Kjölur plateau

Vent at Hveravellir

through a number of grazing meadows. Legend has it that one year four shepherds and their sheep perished in a storm as they crossed the mountains. Their bones were found years later. The hill near the disaster was named Beinahóll or 'Bone Hill'.

The track is named after the 700-m (2,300-ft) high **Kjölur** plateau, set between the Langjökull and Hofsjökull glaciers, whose two similar-sized ice-caps dominate the surrounding landscape.

Start this tour at ★★ **Gullfoss** (Route 5; *see page 65*). The **Hvítá** river, the power behind this spectacular waterfall, flows out of **Hvítárvatn**, a glacial lake at the foot of **Langjökull**. It is possible to see the lake and its glacial spurs, which extend up to its shores, from the main route and also the somewhat rougher parallel section, which branches off after **Hvítar bridge** (34km/21 miles).

The main route soon reaches its highest point (just over 670m/2,200ft), where a memorial stone (74km/45 miles) has successfully withstood the harshest of weather conditions. This monument, which also serves as a viewing point, commemorates the achievements of Geir Zoëga, an engineer who was for many years in charge of building Iceland's roads.

At the centre of the Kjölur plateau it is easy for travellers to forget the inhospitable climate. ★★ **Hveravellir** geothermal area offers hot springs, even a hot pool for a relaxing soak.

The benefits of this oasis were appreciated in the 18th century. Fjalla Eyvindur and his wife Halla endured a whole winter up here in hiding. This ubiquitous pair of bandits spent much of their life on the run from the authorities. A modest shelter made out of stone and the hot spring that Eyvindur converted into a cooking pot are among the very few man-made sights in this barren, upland terrain.

The northern section is less attractive, as for a long way the route follows a new track through the reservoir basin created for **Blönduvirkjun** hydro-electric power station (161km/100 miles). After crossing the **Blanda** river (180km/112 miles) at about halfway between Blönduós and Varmahlíð *(see page 30)*, you will reach the **Blöndudalur** and then link up with Route 2.

The Sprengisandur Route F26

The Sprengisandur Route usually opens at the beginning of July and two alternative routes, which are even tougher, the F821 to Akureyri and the F752 to Varmahlíð, are accessible two weeks later.

This section has had a bad reputation since the Middle Ages – the capricious weather, robbers and evil spirits all making for a hazardous journey. The 'Sprengisandur song', which tells of a rider's fears of evil forces as he follows the track, is one of the most popular folk songs in Iceland and is often sung when people get together in the evenings.

To reach the starting point for this tour, you will probably have to follow Route 5 *(see page 63)* as far as Þjórsárdalur. The **Sigalda power station** is the latest of three high-output hydro-electric stations that harness the currents of the Þjórsá and Tungnaá rivers, which generate electricity for the Reykjavík area as well as the aluminium smelter in Straumsvík.

The route then runs alongside the western shores of **Þórisvatn**. For the benefit of the power station, this lake has been enlarged from its natural size of about 70 sq.km (27 sq.miles) to almost 90 sq.km (34 sq.miles), making it the largest lake in Iceland.

After crossing the **Kaldakvísl bridge** (78km/48 miles) the road becomes more of a track, not all the rivers and streams are bridged and the vegetation becomes noticeably sparser.

Lichens

69

The green **Nýidalur** (150km/93 miles) is a good starting point for hiking tours, some of which can reach to the edge of the smallish **Tungnafellsjökull** glacier. This oasis marks the start of the ★ **Sprengisandur**, an expanse of moorland some 200 sq.km (75 sq.miles) in area and 700 to 800m (2,300 to 2,600ft) high.

The track passes through long sections of monotonous scree landscape. Just before **Mýri** farmhouse (246km/153 miles) a side road branches off to ★★ **Aldeyjarfoss**, one of the finest waterfalls in Iceland. The **Skjálfandafljót** glacial river cascades 20m (65ft) down a layer of basalt columns. Further north it provides the flow for the ★ **Goðafoss** (234km/145 miles) on Route 2 *(see page 34)*.

Aldeyjarfoss

Steaming glacier at the edge of the Kverkfjöll

Route 7

From the bathing lake in hell to the steaming glacier

Hrossaborg – Her∂ubrei∂ – Askja – Kverkfjöll – Mö∂rudalur (272km/169 miles) *See map on page 26*

Taking in the views

In the northeast, on both sides of the Jökulsá á Fjöllum, the highland area is criss-crossed by a network of tracks but they have been modified in recent years, so up-to-date maps are essential *(see page 85)*. This route follows tracks F88 as well as F910, F902 and F903. They usually open between the middle and end of June. Allow at least two if not three days for this tour.

Three times a week in July and August day trips run to Askja from Mývatn. And 3-day Ice and Fire expeditions run along Route 7 but in the opposite direction. Ask at tourist information offices or BSÍ-Travel *(see page 85)*.

Monitoring exhausts

Leave the Ring Road 7km (4 miles) to the west of Grímssta∂ir *(see Route 2 on page 38)* by the **Hrossaborg** crater. Apart from the challenges presented by lava fields and two sizeable fords, the first hour's driving through the **Ó∂á∂ahraun** wastes would be fairly monotonous were it not for the views of the ever-present ★★ **Her∂ubrei∂**, the 'Queen of the Icelandic mountains'.

This 1,682-m/5,518-ft high table volcano began to form sub-glacially during the last Ice Age. Wherever the ejected lava came into contact with ice and meltwater, it left behind on the steep mountain slopes a loose and porous material that is difficult climb. Only when the ice-cap had pushed about 900m/3,000ft above the surrounding terrain did it form itself into a basalt plateau, dominated by a 150 m/500-ft high volcanic cone with its own crater.

At the foot of Herdubreid lies ★ **Herdubreidarlindir** (60km/37 miles), an oasis of wild flowers. Over 100 plant species have been identified here: you will have to seek out the small, bright blue mountain gentian, whereas it is hard to miss the violet Arctic fireweed and the huge clumps of angelica. Another of the shelters built by the outlaw, Fjalla Eyvindur *(see page 68)*, can be found here.

The next few miles of track pass through a barren lava field scattered with bright chunks of buoyant pumice stone. It was here that NASA astronauts rehearsed their first steps on the moon. Nowhere else on earth has ground conditions so similar to those on the moon.

Beside ★ **Drekagil** (90km/56 miles), the 'Dragon's Gorge', lies the **Dyngjufjöll** volcanic massif, better known as ★★ **Askja**, although this name actually only refers to the huge 40-sq.km (15-sq.mile) caldera at the heart of the Dyngjufjöll. A caldera is what geologists call the depression caused by the collapse of the volcanic cone into the empty magma chamber.

The Víti explosion crater

A track runs from a mountain cabin on Drekagil through the lava to the edge of the huge cauldron (98km/60 miles). A further 30-minute walk along the path takes you to the **Víti** explosion crater. You can climb down the slippery slope into the crater, take a quick dip in the sulphurous, lukewarm water or swim over 'hell', the meaning of Víti.

In 1875 a volcanic eruption led to the formation of a smaller crater inside the larger one, now **Öskjuvatn** lake. In 1907 two German geologists disappeared here. A small memorial stone records their death, as yet unexplained.

Return about 20km (12 miles) and then cross on the F910 to the east bank of Jökulsá á Fjöllum. Soon after the bridge the route turns to the south. ★★ **Kverkfjöll** (172km/107 miles) is visible from a long way off. Reaching an altitude of 1,929m (6,328ft), this massif on the north side of Vatnajökull, situated between the two huge valley glaciers of **Dyngjujökull** in the west and **Brúarjökull** in the east, is itself split by a glacial tongue, **Kverkjökull**. Steam from hot sulphurous springs emerges from the edge of the ice or forms bizarre caves. The layout changes year by year.

Kverkfjöll

To enjoy some breathtaking views over the glaciers in the south and the barren uplands in the north, it is possible to climb over the ice into the summit region, but only in the company of an experienced guide.

On the return journey to the Ring Road, you will come across another green oasis in the heart of a seemingly endless wilderness. **Hvannalindir** (200km/124 miles) was also used by Fjalla Eyvindur as a hideout.

Rejoin the Ring Road near **Mödradalur** (272km/169 miles; *see Route 2 on page 39.*

Literature and Music

Small country – great writing

The poetry and prose of medieval Iceland are the country's most important contribution to European culture. The early Germanic epics such as the *Niebelunglied* have clear similarities in form, subject matter and characterisation with the Eddic poems.

The Family Sagas *(see page 13)* are magnificent stories about Iceland and Icelandic heroes from the Viking era, while the Kings' Sagas deal mainly with the background to the Norwegian rulers, but also with events in Denmark, the Faroe Islands, the Orkney Islands and the Baltic. The Icelandic sagas form the core of early medieval Nordic literature. Even during the colonial era, storytelling and the writing of prose and poetry were encouraged.

Njáll the Wise

In the 20th century, new Icelandic writers found recognition in the English-speaking world, notably Halldór Laxness (1902–98), awarded the Nobel prize for literature in 1955. In his early years Laxness travelled widely, spending time in Germany then living in a monastery in Luxembourg, where he wrote his novel *Under the Holy Mountain*, before going to Canada and the US in 1927–30 where he became involved in the Hollywood film industry and converted to Socialism. His fiction writing rejuvenated Icelandic prose and he turned out a series of incomparable epic novels such as *Independent People*, which describes the harsh conditions under which many Icelanders lived, *Christianity at the Glacier, The Fish Can Sing* and *The Atom Station*. A book by Laxness is always a good companion when visiting Iceland.

Halldór Laxnes

73

Younger writers found it hard to match up to Laxness's fame, but slowly they gained recognition and some of their works have been translated into English. These include Einar Már Gudmundsson (b. 1954; *Angels of the Universe*, 1998), Thor Vilhjálmsson (b. 1925; *Justice Undone*, 1998), winner of the Nordic Council's prestigious literature prize, Gudbergur Bergsson (b. 1932; *The Swan*, 1998) and Einar Heimisson (b. 1966), whose novel, *Maria* (1993), now made into a film, describes the fate of Jews who emigrated to Iceland from Nazi Germany. War and its chaos also play a central role in the psychological thriller *Absolution* by Ólafur Jóhann Ólafsson (b. 1962).

The changes that occurred during the 1940s with Iceland occupied by American soldiers and subsequently forced to come out of isolation are described by Einar Kárason (b. 1955) in his brilliant trilogy *Devil's Island, The Isle of Gold* and *The Promised Land*. The books are centred on a colourful family that keeps landing on its feet. In 1992, Kárason wrote *The Wisdom of Fools*, another lively tale that follows the bizarre members of the Schrott-

Fúsi family through Iceland's economic boom years. Iceland's 300 or so modern poets have also been very productive and their works are published regularly.

Music

Ice Pop

Icelandic singers have been acclaimed in opera houses and concert halls throughout the world, but until recently little of the country's own music had reached audiences outside Iceland. Jón Leifs and Atli Heimir Sveinsson, both composers of electronic music, are now well known in Europe. At the end of the 1970s the pop group Mezzoforte made an international breakthrough. They were followed 10 years later by the Sugarcubes. Their lead singer, Björk, has since become one of Iceland's most famous exports. Her albums *Debut* (1993), *Post* (1995) and *Homogenic* (1997) became world bestsellers. Björk's reputation has helped other representatives of 'Ice Pop' on to the world stage. Gus Gus are an accomplished techno group and Páll Oscar, Iceland's representative in the 1996 Eurovision Song Contest, is a leading figure in the gay movement.

74

Cinema

Icelandic film makers have never enjoyed worldwide box office success, but at international festivals Icelandic films regularly get good reviews. The leading producer is undoubtedly Friðrik Þor Friðriksson, whose *Children of Nature* was nominated for an Oscar in 1992 as the best non-English language film of the year. With *Movie Days (1994)*, he won several awards and has enjoyed some success in Europe with *Cold Fever* (1994) and *Devil's Island* (1996) after the novel by E. Kárason. In 2000 he made a film of Einar Már Guðmundsson's *Angels of the Universe*.

Other art forms

Sculpture by Ásmundur Sveinsson

For centuries the written and spoken word overshadowed all other art forms. A long tradition of **handicrafts**, mainly woodcarving, is well documented in Reykjavík's National Museum. But the plastic and performing arts received little public acknowledgement until the 20th century. A **theatre** club was founded in Reykjavík in 1897.

A few young **painters** and **sculptors** returned to their homeland after training at the Art Academy in Copenhagen. Jóhannes S. Kjarval (1885–1972) produced landscape paintings that attracted attention in international artistic circles. The first Icelandic sculptor of note was Einar Jónsson (1874–1954), whose home near Reykjavík's Hallgrímskirkja is now a museum. The same is true of the workshops where Ásmundur Sveinsson (1893–1982) and Sigurjón Ólafsson (1908–82) worked. The best-known contemporary painter is the pop artist, Guðmundur Guðmundsson (b. 1932). Professionally he is known as Erró.

Events Calendar

Reykjavík on New Year's Eve

An Arts Festival is held in Reykjavík in every even-numbered year. It lasts from the end of May to the middle of June and consists mainly of plays and concerts. This biennial event is the largest, regular festival in Iceland.

75

Icelanders love their horses

In the second half of June, a jazz festival attracts an internationally acclaimed celebrity and many Icelandic musicians to Egilsstaðir *(see page 40)*.

In July and August traditional riding events take place. These culminate every two years (2000, 2002, etc.) in the *Landsmót*, a sort of Olympiad for Icelandic horses.

Traditional costume

The first weekend in August, extended by a non-working Monday, Icelanders love to get away from the towns and head for the countryside, preferably one of the few camp-sites in the woodland regions. If you want peace and quiet this weekend, you are most likely to find it in Reykjavík. A traditional celebration is usually held on this date in Her-jólfsdalur on the island of Heimaey *(see page 50)*.

During the second half of September, the farmers drive the sheep and horses down from the summer pastures all together, and a colourful spectacle occurs when the stock is distributed among the various owners. To complete the celebrations, a party is held in the nearest community centre. For many rural areas, this is the most important social event of the year.

The official Christmas celebrations begin at 6pm on December 24. Many people then head off to Mass before going home to a festive dinner, followed by the opening of presents and dancing around the tree. The immediate family tends to be together on Christmas Eve, while Christmas Day is typically reserved for the extended family.

On New Year's Eve there's a *brenna* – a huge bonfire lit to symbolise the burning of the old, followed later in the night by millions of króna's worth of fireworks.

Food and Drink

Icelandic specialities

Gnawing at half a singed and boiled sheep's head, known as *svið*, and taking particular pleasure over the eyes is a gastronomic experience best left to the Icelandic people. Fermented shark or *hákarl* is another local delicacy that is unlikely to whet the appetite, but for those who insist on copying the natives then it should be eaten in small bites and served with a glass of *brennivín*. Pickling in whey is an ancient form of preserving food. The result can be sampled as *blóðmör* and *lifrarpylsa*, black sausage and liver sausage made from sheep. Another example is *hrútspungur* – pickled ram's testicles compressed into a cake.

Seal meat is still on some rural menus

Visitors rarely encounter such unusual traditional delicacies. There are, however, plenty of Icelandic specialities that will pose no problem for the traveller keen to sample true Icelandic fare. Salted fish is prepared in such a way that hardly anyone would notice that it is not fresh. *Hangikjöt* or hung meat is normally smoked lamb, which can be served either as a main course or as charcuterie.

Ptarmigan, puffin and guillemot have been served on Icelandic plates for hundreds of years. *Rúgbrauð*, is a sweetish, brown to brown-black bread. Traditionally, it is prepared in a hot spring, but nowadays the dough is usually cooked by the baker in a *bain-marie*.

Buffet lunch

77

You will come across two types of dairy product. *Skyr* is a type of low-fat soft cheese, usually mixed with fruit or else eaten on its own or perhaps with a little milk and sugar; *súrmjólk* is the delicious thick sour milk that tastes best with brown sugar or added fruit.

In many restaurants, even outside the capital, chefs are now much more likely to experiment and prepare sophisticated food in line with current fashion. Tourists tend to prefer lamb and fish and only top quality, fresh ingredients are used. If an exotic looking deep-sea fish that you have never seen before arrives on the table, then do give it a try. When eating lamb, remember that the animal spent the summer in the uplands grazing on wild herbs, so it will not need any further seasoning.

Prices in good restaurants are comparable with those in European restaurants. Generally, fish is considerably cheaper than meat. Lunchtime meals are better value than the evening menu. Some restaurants have tourist menus or *sumarréttir* (starter, main course, coffee), but it's worth asking the waiter what's on 'today's menu' as it's likely to be written on a chalkboard on the wall in Icelandic.

With décor and marketing in 1960s style, the Icelandic **Pizza '67** chain serve thickly topped but affordable pizzas. These outlets provide good competition in a sector of the market dominated by American fast-food giants.

Alcoholic drinks

Several good varieties of schnaps, known to Icelanders as *brennivín*, are distilled in Iceland. They include the popular brand known as Black Death, which is so named because of the black label.

After the legalisation of beer in 1989, the Icelanders quickly learnt the skills of brewing. Many beers are imported, but local varieties such as Egils, Viking and international brands such as Tuborg dominate the market

Quenching the thirst

The sale of alcoholic drinks, including beer stronger than 2 percent proof, is allowed only from state-run ATVR shops, as well as in restaurants, bars and bistro-style cafés, which must have a special licence. Fast-food restaurants, cafeterias, guesthouses and bed and breakfasts are not normally allowed to serve alcohol.

Visitors from Europe and North America will be unfamiliar with the pricing structure used in Iceland. The drinks sold in the ATVR shops are much dearer than at home. The higher the quality, the smaller the price difference. Prices of long drinks and spirits are more in line with those of mainland Europe, while beer and wine served in restaurants are very expensive. However, most bars and restaurants have special offers on beer.

Kaffi Reykjavík

Restaurant selection

The following are suggestions for Reykjavík and Akureyri. They are listed according to three categories: $$$ = expensive, $$ = moderate, $ = inexpensive.

Reykjavík
Apótekið, Pósthússtræti 16, tel: 575 7900. Right in the centre close to Hotel Borg, this is the new 'grand' upmarket restaurant in Reykjavik. $$$.
Argentína, Barónstíg 11A, tel: 551 9555. Classic steak restaurant with a cigar and cognac lounge. $$$.
Café Ópera, Lækjargötu 2, tel: 552 9499. Rich in atmosphere, fish and steak are served on hot stones at your table. You cook to your desired tenderness. $$$
Café Paris, corner of Pósthússtræti and Austurvöllur, tel: 551 1020. A very pleasant café serving light meals and snacks.
Café Victor, Hafnarstræti 1–3, tel: 561 9555. A lively restaurant/bar with a reasonably priced selection of dishes. Ask what's on today's menu – it will most likely be fresh fish. Situated next to the Irish pub for some lively drinking companions. $
Fjörukráin, Strandgötu 55, tel: 565 1213. This restaurant is in Hafnarfjördur, a suburb to Reykjavik. A taxi ride away but an unforgettable experience of a Viking-Age feast. $$$.
Grænn kostur, Skólavördustig 8 tel: 552 2028. An inexpensive vegetarian restaurant with a hint of spice. $

Seafood galore

Hornid, Hafnarstræti 15, tel: 5551 3340. Popular pizzeria with a cellar bar. Virtually an institution. $$.

Humarhúsid, Amtmannstíg 1 tel: 561 3303. Romantic setting in a house that was the home and office of the Danish King's governor. Emphasis on lobster and fish. $$$

Ítalía, Laugavegi 11, tel: 552 4630. Classic Italian restaurant, never goes wrong. $$

Jómfrúin the Virgin, Lækjargötu 4. tel: 551 0100. Danish restaurant with 120 types of open sandwiches. Best known for Saturday and Sunday brunch. $

Jónatan Livingston Mávur, Tryggvagata 4-6, tel: 551 5520. Fashionable restaurant noted for its fish dishes. $$$.

Kaffi Reykjavík, Vesturgata 2, tel: 562 5540. Fine international cuisine, a wonderful warm atmosphere. $$.

Lækjarbrekka, Bankastræti 2, tel: 551 4430. In a central position, a romantic setting both inside and outside. Good value for money. $$–$$$.

Naust, Vesturgata 6, tel: 551 7759. Traditional fish restaurant in one of the smartest inner-city quarters. $$–$$$.

Á næstu grösum, Laugavegur 26b, tel: 552 8410. Small vegetarian restaurant. $$.

Rex Bar, Austurstræti 9, tel: 551 9111. Trendy and stylishly done right from the cigar cabinet in the cellar to the last candelabra. Innovative, international cuisine. $$$.

Tveir fiskar, Geirsgötu 9, tel: 511 3474. New fish restaurant on the harbour. Best sushi in Reykjavik. $$$

Vid tjörnina, Templarasund 3, tel: 551 8666. Furnished in 1920s style, but with modern, innovative cuisine. $$–$$$.

Chefs at the Lækjarbrekka

Akureyri

Smidjan/Bautinn, Hafnarstræti 92 (opposite Hótel KEA), tel: 462 1818. Two restaurants under one roof: Smidjan is the town's top restaurant ($$$) opening on to the fjord. Bautinn is a bistro-style restaurant with good value lunchtime dishes ($–$$).

Við Pollinn, Strandgata 49, tel: 461 2757. Lively bar. $$.
Súlnaberg, Hafnarstræti 89, tel: 462 2200. Cafeteria for those on a tight budget. $.
Veitingahúsið Brekka, Hrísey island, tel: 466 1751 (also hotel). Steakhouse on the fjord island of Hrísey. $$.

Many bars have live music

A night out in Reykjavík

Reykjavík can boast almost 100 pubs, bars and fashionable bistros. Most bars are on Laugavegur, the little side streets of Laugavegur and down the hill towards the centre. Icelanders go out to bars around midnight and on Fridays and Saturdays clubs can stay open till the early hours of the morning. Here is a selection:

Cafe '22', Laugavegur 22, has a pub-style bar downstairs and at weekends there is dancing upstairs; popular late at night. **Café List**, Laugavegur 20, is the Spanish tapas bar in Reykjavík. It turns wild after midnight with the art and theatre crowd. **Kaffibarinn** just up from the corner of Laugavegur 12 is a small bar popular from early evening and well into the next morning; Damon Albarn from the pop group Blur owns a stake here. **Tres Locos** on the other corner is a popular Mexican bar. Next corner down is **Kofi Tómasar frænda** (Uncle Tom's Cabin), more Uncle Tom's basement but attracting the younger crowd for beer or strong coffee. On the next corner at Bankastræti 7, **Café Sólon Íslandus** is an upmarket café that turns into a lively bar in the evenings. Nearby **Café Prikið** operates in various guises from 7am to dawn.

A night at the Astro

Down Ingólfsstræti turning left into Hverfisgata, you arrive at **Spotlight**, a gay/mixed dance club open Thursday, Friday and Saturday nights. **Nelly's Café** is on the next corner down the hill; it is popular every evening mainly because of its cheap beer (prices go up after 1am at weekends). Down the hill after the crossroads you have **Wunderbar** at Lækjargata 2, a good place to drink and eat snacks. Around the corner into Austurstræti is **Astro Club**, a serious dance club for the young, beautiful and fashionable open at weekends. Across the square at Hafnarstræti 17 is **Kaffi Thomsen**, a hardcore dance club with first-rate DJs and visiting celebs. Go back to Austurstræti where at **Rex Number 9** you find a cool restaurant/bar designed by the Terence Conran team. Pósthússtræti leads off Austurstræti. Adjacent to Hotel Borg at Pósthússtræti 11 is the **Skuggabarinn** (The Shadow Bar) – very popular with the 'well off'. To the left of Hotel Borg you have **Kaffibrennslan** where most night owls stop for a beer early on to check out where the crowd is heading. Some stay open all night. And finally don't forget to pay homage to **Dubliners** at Hafnarstræti 4, an authentic Irish pub, and **Gaukur á Stöng**, Tryggvagata 22, who got the beer legalisation ball rolling with its beer cocktails. Very noisy.

Active Holidays

Riders, anglers and walkers will be in their element in Iceland. Golfers can indulge in their favourite sport until midnight, while mountain bikers can test themselves to the limit on the steep hillsides. More and more glacier regions offer winter sports in the summer. Canoeing and river rafting on torrential glacial rivers are increasingly popular and, thanks to the endless supply of hot water from underground, Iceland is an open-air swimming pool all year.

Angling is a popular pastime. A licence is needed for all inland waters and this can be expensive where salmon are fished. Expect to pay about £7 a day in trout waters.

Among Iceland's **golf** courses the US magazine *Golf Weekly* rates the Leirur golf course near Keflavík very highly. The Arctic Open Championship is held in June under the midnight sun. For information and registration contact Akureyri Golf Club, tel: 462 2974, fax: 461 1755.

To go **mountain biking** on Iceland's rough tracks must be the dream of all off-road cyclists, even though you can't cylce freely everywhere. Organised tours for small groups arrange for luggage to be taken ahead and the uninteresting sections are covered by bus.

Riding ranges from hour-long sessions or half-day excursions on the outskirts of Reykjavík to two-week trails through the highlands. Also on offer are upland rides, breaking in young horses in the spring, driving semi-wild horses up to the meadows at the start of summer or back down as winter approaches, etc. Contact **Arinbjörn Jóhannsson**, Brekkulækur, IS-531 Hvammstangi, tel: 451 2938, fax: 451 2998, e-mail: brekka@nett.is.

Out riding

To go **walking** or **trekking**, you will need sturdy footwear, equipment that is suitable for all weathers, a high level of fitness and experience in difficult terrain. This is particularly important for the highland tours. For walking tours with Icelanders contact Ferðafélag Íslands or Útivist walking clubs *(for addresses see Cabins, page 96)*.

Winter sports are possible in summer on several glaciers and in the Kerlingarfjöll. Winter ski areas are Bláfjöll, 20km (12 miles) southeast of Reykjavík, Hengill near the Ring Road towards Hveragerði, and Skálafell in the Esja mountains. Ísafjörður and Akureyri also have good ski areas. In winter in Hellisheiði, on the outskirts of Reykjavík, and in summer from Myrdalsjökull, Geysir Snowmobil Expeditions (Dugguvogur 10, IS-104 Reykjavík, tel: 568 8888, fax: 581 3102) organise skidoo excursions.

Negotiating a stream

Take a skidoo

River rafting is about gliding down fast-flowing glacial rivers in dinghies, for example on the Hvítá river below Gullfoss *(see page 65)*; day trips from Reykjavík and on rivers in the Skagafjörður hinterland *(see page 30)*. Reservations via BSÍ Travel *(see page 85)*.

Getting There

By air

Icelandair (www.icelandair.net) is the main carrier operating regular scheduled flights from Europe and North America to Iceland: (all year) London, Glasgow, Copenhagen, Oslo, Stockholm, Amsterdam, Hamburg, Frankfurt, Paris, Halifax, Boston, New York, Orlando, Baltimore, Minneapolis, Faroe Islands and Greenland; (summer) Barcelona, Milan, Zurich and Cologne.

Icelandair UK: 172 Tottenham Court Road, 3rd floor, London W1P 9LG, tel: 020 7874 1000; fax: 020 7387 5711. **US**: 5950 Symphony Woods Road, Suite 410, Columbia MD 21044, tel: 410 715 1600, fax: 410 715 3548.

Travellers from the UK have the option of flying with the low-cost subsidiary of British Airways, **Go Airlines** (tel: 0845 605 4321; www.go-fly.com), which offers very reasonably priced flights from London Stansted. In addition, there are a number of Icelandic tour operators that sell tickets on various charters:

Samvinn Travel, Sætuni 1, Reykjavík, tel: 569 1010; www.samvinn.is. Large tour operator with flights from many European cities; **Heimsferðir**, Austurstræti 17, Reykjavík, tel: 595 1000; www.heimsferdir.is; **Terra Nova**, Stangarhyl 3a, Reykjavík, tel: 567 8545; www.terranova.is.

Iceland's international airport, Leifur Eiríksson, is situated 45km (28 miles) southwest of Reykjavík near Keflavík. A connecting bus service links the airport with the air terminal at Icelandair Hótel Loftleiðir in Reykjavík. Onward transfer can be arranged to the major hotels.

Arriving by air

83

By boat

Leaving Seydisfjordur

A Faroese ferry company, Smyril Line, operates a weekly service from mid-May to mid-September between mainland Europe and Iceland (Seyðisfjorður). The ferry takes a zigzag route from Hanstholm in northern Denmark, calling in at the Faroe Islands, the Shetland Islands and Norway. The journey from Denmark to Iceland or from Iceland to the Shetland Islands and Norway (only in these directions) involves a two- or three-day stay on the Faroe Islands.

Container ships belonging to the Icelandic shipping company, Eimskip, cover the route from Iceland to mainland Europe all year round. They carry up to 12 passengers. It is possible to send a vehicle as freight, but fly direct.

Smyril Line email: marketing@smyrilline.fo; website: www.smyril-line.fo. In Faroes: J. Bronsksgota 37, PO Box 370, FR-110 Tórshavn, tel: 298-315 900.

Eimskip email: info@eimskip.com; website: www.eimskip.com. Alternatively, contact Iceland Travel, Lágmúli 4, 108 Reykavík, tel: 585 4000; fax: 588 0202.

Glacier by bus

Getting Around

Bus, plane or car?

Choosing which form of transport to use is no easy task, as there are many options. The choices available between Reykjavík and Akureyri, Iceland's two main towns, demonstrate the point. If you travel one way between the two towns on a scheduled bus along the Ring Road (389km/242 miles), it will cost about £40 (US$60). Take the bus cross-country along the Kjölur route *(see page 67)*, then the fare will be about £50 ($75), but then a one-way flight at the normal tariff will probably cost less than £45 ($65), a return about £75 ($110). Families, students and senior citizens are entitled to further reductions. To travel one way by air and one way by bus (Air-Bus-Rover tickets) will cost £80–£90 ($120+), depending on whether the bus takes the Ring Road or the cross-country route. A small hire car will cost anything from £40 to £100 ($60–150) for a day, plus fuel. Cheaper rates for tourists apply if the car is booked for longer periods or in advance.

Heading through the Jökulsárgljúfur

By bus

Buses run to all inhabited parts of the country. During the summer they operate along the full length of the Ring Road every day, some sections of it several times a day. In sparsely populated regions and outside the summer season, the services are irregular. From the beginning of October until mid-May the eastern section of the Ring Road is not passable after Höfn.

A number of one-day or multi-day excursions are based around the scheduled bus services, i.e. in combination with other forms of transport (ferries, flights). The Air-Bus-Rover tickets are particularly good value. You can travel one way by air, the other way by bus. If you want to rely entirely on buses, then you can buy a bus pass for a full tour of the island (more expensive if including the West-fjords) or for unlimited bus travel (for one week or for four weeks) or the Highland Pass, which reduces the fares for the highland buses.

There are also many guided coach tours. Independent travellers should make further inquiries at **BSÍ Travel**, Vatnsmýrarvegur 10, 101 Reykjavík, tel: 552 2300, fax: 552 9973; website: www.bsi.is.

By air

Two companies serve about a dozen places throughout Iceland from Reykjavík's city airport:

Flugfélag Íslands (Icelandair's subsidiary company for domestic flights), 101 Reykjavík, tel: 570 3030, fax: 570 3001 operates from a terminal at the western end of the airfield; from Akureyri there are onward flights to smaller towns in the northeast of Iceland, to the Arctic Circle island of Grímsey and to Ísafjör]ur and Egilsstaðir.

Íslandsflug (101 Reykjavík, tel: 570 8090, fax: 570 8091) has a terminal near the Icelandair Hótel Loftleiðir at the eastern end of the airport. The airline has recently cut down its domestic operation, but still flies from Reykjavík to Sauðárkrókur, Siglufjörður and Vesturbyggd.

Both airlines provide good value air passes for tourists, e.g. Flugfélag Íslands 12 days of unlimited flights (reservations only from outside Iceland) and adventure day trips from Reykjavík including glacier tours.

By ferry

For ferry connections *see below*. There is a connection to the Westman Islands from Þorlákshöfn (1–2 times daily; bus from/to Reykjavík). Reservations from tourist information offices or BSÍ Travel *(see above)*.

By car

Iceland's roads, once notorious for their extremely poor quality, are now mainly asphalt. Where the surface is still gravel, then drivers must, of course, take great care. Speed is the greatest risk when driving on loose surfaces. Under no circumstances should a vehicle's undercarriage clearance be restricted by overloading.

An important item for independent drivers is, of course, a good road map. The Iceland Geodetic Survey's Landmælingar Íslands and Mal og Menning Publishers both produce maps of Iceland. These detailed maps show how the asphalting is progressing and also the ever-changing course of the highland tracks.

All the usual car hire companies have offices in Reykjavík and the surrounding area. Hertz (in co-operation with Icelandair) and Europcar have offices in other towns. Most

85

Each season has its own hazards

Iceland tour operators offer car hire packages based on 100, 200 or unlimited kilometres, including fully comprehensive insurance and VAT or else fly-drive deals. Whether it is better to book in advance or when you arrive in Iceland depends, to some extent, on the current rate of exchange, but remember that during the summer not all types of vehicles are available at short notice. For travelling around the coast a car is perfectly adequate, but anyone contemplating a trip into the interior will need a 4WD vehicle. (Insurance companies will not cover hire cars taken into the interior.)

An all-inclusive package for a smaller vehicle during the summer will cost £40–£100 (US$60–150) a day, a little less for an extended period; the smallest 4WD vehicle £85–£130 ($120–190) a day, again a little less for an extended hire period. One-way rentals are very expensive, unless you want an ordinary saloon car for a journey between two main towns and it is hired from one of the main companies. Many hire companies make a surcharge for collection/return at Keflavík airport.

Petrol is expensive in Iceland (approximately ISK 90 per litre). There are plenty of places to buy fuel. Where no fuel is available for long stretches of road, roadside signs keep motorists informed. Diesel-powered vehicles are, however, heavily taxed. Tourists bringing in diesel vehicles will be charged according to weight.

Travelling in the highlands

The vegetation in highland areas has only two months each year to grow and so must be treated with great care. It is the duty of every traveller in Iceland to protect and to maintain the natural environment. Always stay on the beaten track. If you damage the topsoil in any way, you have created a weak spot that will be exploited by the destructive power of wind erosion.

Much worse than footsteps are tyre tracks, even those left by mountain bikes. The highlands are no place for off-road enthusiasts. They should stick to the tracks – it would be hard to find tougher road conditions anywhere in Europe. Off-road driving in the true sense of the word is not permitted anywhere in Iceland.

Mind the delicate flora

Leave nature as you find it

- Leave your campsite or service area as you would expect to find it.
- Do not leave any rubbish lying around – and do not bury any either.
- Do not light a fire on vegetation.
- Do not break any stones and do not build stone figures for the fun of it.
- Do not pollute the water.
- Do not damage any plants.

- Do not disturb any animals.
- Do not alter any geological formations.
- Do not make any unnecessary noise.
- Never drive off the track.
- Always follow the signposted footpaths.
- Follow the country code and the instructions of park wardens.

Fording rivers
- Check for any up-to-date information about rivers on your route.
- Never try to ford rivers in vehicles which do not have protected engines.
- If possible ford rivers in convoy, so that help is always at hand.
- Never follow vehicle tracks into a river without checking the spot first.
- Remember: fords can become dangerous at any time.
- Check the depth and current of unknown rivers before crossing.
- Wear warm, bright clothing.

Fords can become dangerous at any time

For routes 6 and 7 (*see pages 67 and 70*) you will need a robust 4WD with plenty of undercarriage clearance. Do not trust any notice which states that certain highland routes are passable in an ordinary saloon car. There are very few days in the year when such conditions exist and a visitor is not in any position to know for certain what lies ahead. Many fatal accidents occur as a result of tourers underestimating road and weather conditions.

Wear bright clothing

Reykjavík

Reykjavík city transport

The central bus stop for city buses is on Lækjargata near the tourist information office and Hlemmur Square. One journey on an SVR bus costs 150 ISK. This has to be counted out for the driver and then thrown into a container. Long-distance buses leave from the BSÍ terminal (Vatnsmyrarvegur) on the north side of the city airport.

For a charge of between 600 and 1,000 ISK, the Reykjavík Tourist Card (from tourist information offices) entitles visitors to three days' unlimited travel on SVR buses and free admission to municipal baths and museums.

Sightseeing tours of the city and excursions into the outlying areas are provided by Reykjavík Excursion, which has an office in Bankastræti 2 (in the same building as the tourist information office), tel: 562 4422.

Akureyri

By air
There are scheduled flights to Reykjavík, Ísafjördur and Egilsstadir, to the island of Grímsey and to other smaller

towns on Iceland's north and northeast coast as well as day trips to eastern Greenland during the summer months.

By bus

There are buses to Reykjavík 1–2 times daily via the Ring Road, in the summer also daily via the highland route; to Dalvík and Ólafsfjörður daily; to Egilsstaðir June–August daily mid-May–mid-October 3 times per week; to Mývatn in high season 1–2 times daily, otherwise 3 times per week; to Húsavík daily, in the summer onward to Ásbyrgi and several times a week around the northeastern islands.

By boat

To Grímsey Island twice a week (day trip with land tour available).

Rock formations at Lake Mývatn; climbing in the Jökulsárgljúfur

Myvatn

Timetabled buses run from Reykjavík to Mývatn via Sprengisandur. Also available are excursions to the main sights around Mývatn, to Askja, Dettifoss and Jökulsárgljúfur National Park (10 hours). Ask at the tourist office or BSÍ-Travel (see page 85).

Egilsstaðir

By air

Scheduled flights to Reykjavík, Akureyri and Höfn and charter flights over the Eastfjords and the northern edge of Vatnajökull.

By bus

The Egilsstaðir–Höfn–Reykjavík bus service follows Route 3 (see page 42). A rather rudimentary and irregular bus service from Egilsstaðir goes to the surrounding area, e.g. Hallormsstaður twice a week, Eiðar twice a week, Seyðisfjörður 1–2 times a day. The range of excursions for independent travellers is rather modest. It is possible to take combined bus/boat tours via Seyðisfjörður or Neskaupstaður to some of the more remote fjords. For up-to-date information ask at the tourist information office or where you are staying.

Höfn

By air

There are scheduled services to and from Reykjavík and Egilsstaðir. The airport is situated about 8km (5 miles) to the northwest of the town. Contact Flugfélag Íslands (tel: 478 1250) for reservations.

By bus

As well as the summer Ring Road service, buses leave daily to the main starting points for tours of Vatnajökull.

Vatnajökull

The Jöklaferðir company arranges glacier tours and excursions by snowmobile or motorised sleigh, including 1-to 2-hour trips close to the Jöklasel base on the **Skálafellsjökull**, whole-day tours and longer crossings of Vatnajökull to Kverkfjöll *(see page 71)*. For further information on any of these, and to make reservations, contact Höfn tourist information office *(see page 91)*.

Snæfellsnes

By bus
Buses for the Snæfellsnes peninsula leave Reykjavík every day. There are connecting excursions around Snæfellsjökull by bus or by boat around the Breiðafjörður islands.

The bus timetable in the Westfjords is restricted to only a few routes on specific days of the week. For journeys between Reykjavík and Ísafjörður, there are connections in Stykkishólmur, Látrabjarg and Hólmavík on the Strandir coast.

BSÍ Travel *(see page 85)* arranges attractively priced package tours by scheduled bus, which include overnight accommodation, to the islands of Flatey and Látrabjarg.

By ferry
The *Baldur* ferry (for bookings call 438 1120, fax: 438 1093) plies between Stykkishólmur and Brjánslækur with a stopover on the island of Flatey 1–2 times daily, journey time about 3 hours. The crossing, which is part of Route 4 *(see page 53)* can be avoided, but the 300-km (185-mile) journey is along poor roads.

By air
Several places along Route 4 are served by flights from Reykjavík, i.e. Flugfélag Íslands for Ísafjörður and Íslandsflug for Vesturbyggd. Flugfélag Íslands also operates a service between Ísafjörður and Akureyri. Sightseeing flights and air excursions with land tours are available to Stykkishólmur, Látrabjarg and Ísafjörður from Reykjavík.

Excursion flights to villages in the Westfjord region and to runways on the Hornstrandir peninsula from Ísafjörður are on a charter basis.

Ísafjörður

The *Fagranes* ferry (tel: 456 3155) runs throughout the year to destinations in Ísafjarðardjúp (vehicles) and during the summer to jetties on the Hornstrandir peninsula (passengers only). Motorboats are also available on a charter basis, and sometimes on a scheduled basis, to other destinations in the region. For more details, ask at Ísafjörður tourist information office *(see page 91)*.

89

Snaefellsnes

Skidoo team

Jökulsárlón memento

Facts for the Visitor

Visas

The citizens of most Western European nations, including the UK, and many other countries, including Australia, New Zealand, Canada and the USA need only a valid passport to enter as tourists.

Customs

Clothing, equipment and vehicles for personal use may be imported free of duty. The following restrictions apply: travellers aged 20 and over, no more than 1 litre of spirits up to 47 percent alcohol content and 1 litre of wine or 1 litre of spirits up to 21 percent alcohol content or 6 litres of imported beer or 8 litres of Icelandic beer.

Travellers aged 16 and over may import 200 cigarettes or 250g tobacco products, preserved food to an upper limit of 3kg per person. Fresh food may not be imported and fuel must be stored in the vehicle's fitted tank. Fishing and riding equipment must be new or there must be documented evidence that it has been disinfected. For a small charge any equipment can be disinfected on arrival.

Find out where to enjoy a good bath

Tourist information

In the UK: 172 Tottenham Court Road, 3rd Floor, London W1P 9LG, tel: 020 7874 1000, fax: 020 7387 5711.
In the US: 655 Third Avenue, New York, NY 10017, tel: 212 949 2333, fax: 212 983 5260.
In Iceland: For Reykjavík and the whole of Iceland: Upplysingamidstöd ferdamála, Bankastræti 2, IS-01 Reykjavík, tel: 562 3045, fax: 562 3057; open 15 May–15 August daily, 8.30am–7pm; for the rest of the year Mon–Fri 9am–5pm, Sat 10am–2pm. Website: www.ice-tourist.is.

*formation desk in the new town hall, tel: 563 2005; open
1on–Fri 8.30am–6pm mid-May to mid-September, also
un noon–6pm.

See also these exciting websites that may help you with
lanning your travels in Iceland: www.discovericeland.is;
ww.icelandcomplete.is; www.reykjavik.is; www.reyk-
vik.com; www.farmholidays.is; www.travelnet.is. Those
search of nightlife in Reykjavík should consider log-
ing on to www.citywalk.is.

ocal tourist offices

he 25-plus tourist information offices throughout
celand supply information about the locality, and in
ome cases the whole country. Practical information and
vents are shown in the free English-language leaflets
round Iceland, *Around Reykjavík* and *What's on in
eykjavík*, available in tourist information offices, hotels,
ostels, etc.

kureyri: Upplýsingamiðstöð, Hafnarstræti 82 (bus sta-
on), IS-600 Akureyri, tel: 462 7733 or 462 4442, fax:
61 1817; 1 June–31 August, Mon–Fri 9am–9pm, Sat and
unday noon–8pm; winter Mon–Fri 8.30am–5pm.
rnastapi: Ferðaþjónustan Snjófell, IS-355 Arnastapi,
el: 435 6783, fax: 453 6795. At the campsite. **Ásbyrgi**:
jaldsvæpi Ásbyrgi campsite, tel: 465 2195. **Djúpivogur**:
lótel Framtíð, tel: 478 8887, fax: 478 8187. **Egilsstaðir**:
aupvangar 10, tel: 471 2320, fax: 471 1707. 1 June to
1 August, daily at least 9am–9pm, otherwise 9am–5pm.
löfn: Travel Center, IS-780 Hornafjörður, tel: 478 1701,
ax: 478 1901. At the campsite. **Húsafell**: Húsafell Ser-
ice Center campsite. **Hveragerði**: Breiðamörk 10, IS-
10 Hveragerði, tel: 483 4280, fax: 483 4287. June–
nid-September, Mon–Fri 9am–6pm, Sat and Sun
am–2pm. **Ísafjörður**: Apalstræti 7, IS-400 Ísafjörpur,
el: 456 5121, fax: 456 5122. Mon–Fri 8am–6pm, sum-
ner also Sat and Sun 10am–2pm. **Þingvellir**: Þingvellir
Travel Center at the national park offices by Highway 36.
el: 482 2660. **Reykjahlíð**: Bjarg/Eldá Travel Services,
el: 464 4220, fax: 464 4321. Tjaldsvældi Reykjahlíð
ampsite, tel: 464 4103, fax: 464 4305. **Sauðárkrókur**:
osshótel Áning, v/Sæmundarhlíp, Sauðárkrókur. **Seyðis-
jörður**: Fjarðagata 8 (by the ferry terminal), tel: 472
111, fax: 472 1105. **Skaftafell National Park**: At the
ampsite, tel: 478 1627, fax: 478 1846. **Staparskáli**:
taparskáli campsite. **Stykkishólmur**: Eyjaferðir, Apal-
ata 2, IS-340 Stykkishólmur, tel: 438 1450, fax: 438
050. The largest travel agency in the area serves both
s a tourist information office and local cruise and coach
perator. **Varmahlíð**: Service area (in summer only). **Vík**:
víkurskáli service area, tel: 487 1230, fax: 487 1302.

*Sculpture near Húsafell
by Pall Guðmundsson*

91

Puffin and friends at Ingólfshöfði

Currency and exchange

The Icelandic unit of currency is the *krónur*, sometimes abbreviated to IsKr, more often now ISK. Banknotes are in denominations of 500, 1,000, 2,000 and 5,000 *krónur*, coins in 1, 5, 10, 50 and 100 *krónur*. 1 *króna* = 100 *aurar*, but the latter are usually rounded up or down and the coins are rarely used nowadays.

It is cheaper to exchange cash in Iceland than abroad. There are no currency restrictions for holidaymakers. Credit cards can be used practically everywhere. Banks and larger hotels accept travellers' cheques. Credit cards are also accepted for small amounts in bars and supermarkets, and even taxis. There are bureaux de change at Keflavík airport and at the ferry terminal in Seyðisfjörður. Many tourist-orientated shops accept foreign banknotes.

Jewellery shop in Reykjavík

92

VAT

VAT in Iceland is 24.5 percent. If you are buying high-value goods (4,000 ISK or more) in shops carrying the 'Europe Tax Free Shopping' sign, about 15 percent of the purchase price can be reclaimed. The money is returned as you leave Iceland from Keflavík airport at a branch of Landsbanki Íslands situated in the transit lounge. If you are leaving Iceland on a ferry or a cruise ship, then ask for further information from the shops participating in the scheme. In any event, your receipt must be stamped by an Icelandic customs official. 'Europe Tax Free Shopping' has about 3,000 outlets throughout Europe, from which the rebate can be collected.

Public holidays

Christmas time

New Year's Day, Maundy Thursday, Good Friday, Easter Sunday, Easter Monday, first day of summer on the third Thursday in April, Labour Day (1 May), Ascension Day, Whit Sunday, Whit Monday, Icelandic National Holiday (17 June), Shop and Office Workers' Holiday on the first Monday in August, Christmas Eve from noon, Christmas Day and Boxing Day, New Year's Eve from noon.

Telephone and fax

When making calls within Iceland, simply dial the seven-figure number. There are no dialling codes. When calling Iceland from Europe, prefix your number with 00 + 354. When dialling home from Iceland, start with 00, dial the country code (e.g. UK = 44, US and Canada = 1), then the area code without the 0, followed by your number. You can make international calls from all telephones. Phone cards are available from post offices.

GSM mobile phones can be used as long as you have had the international roaming bar lifted. Reception now reaches 95 percent of all Icelanders.

Postal services

Almost all towns have a post office and telephone booths (*Póstur og Sími*). Opening times are Mon–Fri 9am–4.30pm, in towns a little longer. The rate for letters and postcards to Europe is 50 ISK.

Tipping

It is not normal to tip in restaurants and cafés, but it is usual to offer a small gratuity to the drivers and guides responsible for sightseeing tours.

Time

Greenwich Mean Time applies throughout Iceland all-year-round.

Electricity

The voltage in Iceland is 220V. Continental-style sockets are used, so adapters are needed for UK and US plugs.

Opening times

Shop opening times are largely unrestricted. Core times are as follows: Mon–Fri 9am–6pm, Sat 10am–4pm. Kiosks at petrol stations in rural areas sell a wide range of goods and stay open until late at night.

Banks: Mon–Fri 9.15am–4pm. Extended opening times at Keflavík airport and the tourist information office in Reykjavík (Bankastræti 2).

Souvenirs

Classic souvenirs from Iceland are wool and woollen products in traditional or modern designs. The best place to buy such items is one of the shops belonging to the rural women's co-operative. Craft shops often sell innovative jewellery, glass and ceramic pieces. Fish and lamb, vacuum-packed or conserved in some other way, are sold in the duty-free shop at Keflavík airport.

Clothing and equipment

Waterproofs are essential

Wind- and rainproof jackets and trousers are essential. You should have at least one pair of shoes or walking boots that cover the ankles. Rubber sandals or an old pair of trainers, together with a telescopic walking pole, are helpful when crossing rivers. If you intend to camp, take with you the best quality sleeping bag, tent and insulated ground mat you can afford.

Traffic regulations

Icelandic traffic regulations are basically the same as the rest of Europe. Traffic and warning signs are few and far between but, where they do exist, they must always be heeded, particularly the one marked *Blindhæðir*, which

Heed the signs

warns of blind spots on narrow roads. The maximum speed in towns is 50km/h (30mph), outside built-up areas on gravel roads 80km/h (50mph), 90km/h (55mph) on asphalt roads. Seat belts must be worn front and back and headlights switched on at all times. Drink-driving laws are strictly enforced. The blood alcohol limit is 0.05 percent. When animals and cars meet, the vehicle driver is liable to compensation claims by the owner of the animal.

Mind the horses

Photography

Films for cameras and video equipment are widely available, but expensive. Some museums forbid photography. It is illegal to photograph protected birds in their nest.

Medical

Medical provision in Iceland is very good. All larger towns have hospitals or health centres. Look in the inside cover of the telephone directory under *Læknavakt* (emergency doctor) and *Sjúkrahús* (hospital).

Health and insurance

Visitors to Iceland should take out an accident and illness insurance policy that will meet the full extent of any claim. Travellers from EU countries can present the E111 certificate, which entitles holders to the benefits of the Icelandic health service at the same rates as native Icelanders. However, this usually involves a hefty private contribution, e.g. for dental treatment and medications.

Insure against salvage

If you are bringing your car to Iceland, then you must insure against salvage and transport costs. Even write-offs have to be exported or incur heavy import duties.

Emergency numbers

Emergency *(Neyðarsími)*: tel: 112. Other numbers on the inside cover of the telephone directory: Fire *(Slökkvistöð)*; Police *(Lögregla)*; Ambulance *(Sjúkrabíll)*; Emergency doctor *(Læknavakt)*; Hospital *(Sjúkrahús)*.

Lost and found

Ask at the nearest police station

Disabled

In remote areas accommodation and washing facilities adapted for the disabled are not generally available. Hotel listings give information on amenities for the disabled.

Ferðafélagar hf, Reynigrund 65, IS-200 Kópavogur, tel: 564 4091, fax: 564 4092, runs tours for disabled groups.

Diplomatic representation

Great Britain: Laufásvegur 31, tel: 550 5100.
US: Laufásvegur 21, tel: 562 9100.

Accommodation

Camping in the mountains

Iceland has over 100 hotels and guesthouses, ranging from simple country hotels and boarding schools converted into hostels to luxury accommodation with all mod cons. In addition, there are over 100 farmhouses, 25 youth hostels, 34 mountain cabins belonging to both walking clubs *(see page 96),* countless sleeping bag cabins for backpackers and more than 120 campsites. Some hotels and guesthouses have cheap dormitories with either made-up beds or mattresses for sleeping bags. Accommodation vouchers are not always better value than cash. As it is not possible to make advance reservations with vouchers, they are not a lot of use if at the end of a long day's hiking, the hotel for which the voucher is valid has no beds. Unused vouchers are normally only reimbursed at 80 percent.

The rooftops of Reykjavík

Hotels are priced as follows: $$$ expensive; $$ moderate; $ basic.

Hotel chains

Fosshótels, Skipholt 50c, IS-105 Reykjavík, tel: 562 4000, fax: 562 4001, www.fosshotel.is. Good tourist hotels of varying standards; six are open all year round, four in summer only. $–$$$.

  Icelandair Hotels, c/o Hotel Loftleidir, IS-101 Reykjavík, tel: 505 0900, fax: 505 0905, www.icehotels.is. Six hotels open all year, comfortable, $$–$$$.

  Edda Hotels, www.hoteledda.is. A chain of nice hotels around the country. Some are open all year round and some are open in the summer only. A few are operated in boarding schools that are on vacation, $–$$.

  Key Hotels, c/o Hotel Cabin, Borgartun 32, IS-105 Reykjavík, tel: 511 6030, fax: 511 6031. Tourist hotels of varying standards, four open all year, two summer only. ($–$$$); good-value vouchers for seven-night stays. ($).

Rainbow Hotels, c/o Hotel Borgarnes, tel: 437 1119, fax: 437 1443. Good quality hotels in various locations around the country. $$–$$$.

Guesthouses

These offer an inexpensive alternative to hotels, mainly in the towns (usually $). Generally only breakfast available.

Farmhouses

Farmhouses provide bed and breakfast and other meals on request. Many belong to the Farmhouse Holidays organisation. Information from Ferðþjónusta Bænda, Hafnarstræti 1, IS-101 Reykjavík, tel: 562 3640, fax: 562 3644, www.sveit.is or farmholidays.is. Not all farmhouses accept vouchers; some farmers accept lower prices for cash. The same applies to vouchers for sleeping-bag cabins on farms.

Youth hostels

Youth hostels accept all guests with no age limit. Among the 25-plus hostels (most open only in summer) are farmhouses, clubhouses and schools, all with cooking facilities for guests. Many offer double rooms, but combined accommodation for men and women is the rule rather than the exception. The atmosphere is relaxed. An overnight stay costs about £8 (US$12) for Youth Hostel Association members. Bed-linen, available for hire, or a sleeping bag are required. Information from Bandalag Íslenskra Farfugla, Sundlaugavegur 34, IS-105 Reykjavík, tel: 553 8110, fax: 588 9201. Youth hostel vouchers cost over £10 ($15).

Cabins

Free sleeping-bag cabins (for backpackers) are as varied

Types of cabin

as the youth hostels; not all have cooking facilities.

Non-members may use **hiking club cabins** in the island's interior. These mattress camps cost £7–£10 ($10–15) a night. It is best to bring your own food and a stove to cook it. In summer a pre-payment and reservation is essential through one of the club offices: Ferðafélag Íslands, Mörkin 6, IS-108 Reykjavík, tel: 568 2533, fax: 568 2535; Útivist, Hallveigarstígur 1, IS-101 Reykjavík, tel: 561 4330, fax: 561 4606. Orange emergency cabins are not for tourists' use, private cabins only with the owner's permission.

Campsites

Campsites can be found in almost every district, in all national parks and near popular sightseeing areas. Camping is permitted only within fenced-off or attended spaces, provided the landowner is in agreement. Camping is often free at the most basic of sites; otherwise, expect to pay £2–£5 ($3–7.50) per person per night. A directory of campsites is available from the Icelandic Tourist Board *(see page 90)*.

Hotel selection

The following are suggestions for the main destinations in this guide. They are listed according to three categories: $$$ = expensive, $$ = moderate, $ = inexpensive.

Reykjavík

Hótel Borg, Pósthússtræti 11, PO Box 200, IS-101 Reykjavík, tel: 551 1440, fax: 551 1420; www.hotel-borg.is. Grand hotel in the old-style. Intimate setting with only a few rooms; plenty of atmosphere. One of northern Europe's finest hotels. $$$.

Hótel Holt, Bergstaðastræti 37, IS-101 Reykjavík, tel: 552 5700, fax: 562 3025; www.holt.is. Great food, excellent game dishes, and one of Iceland's best art collections. $$$.

Hótel Saga, Hagatorg, tel: 525 9900, fax: 525 9929, www.hotelsaga.is. A top-class hotel not far from the city centre and next door to the University Theatre. One of the best restaurants in the country on the top floor. $$$.

Fosshótel Lind, Rauðarástigur 18, 1S-105 Reykjavík, tel: 562 3350, fax: 562 3351, www.fosshotel.is. Tourist hotel near Hlemmur Square. $$–$$$.

Hótel Borg (above) and Hótel Saga

Icelandair Hótel Loftleiðir, v/Hlíðarfót, IS-101 Reykjavík, tel: 505 0900, fax: 505 0905; www.icehotels.is. A 220-room hotel near the city airport; business/conference facilities. $$–$$$.

Hotel Skjaldbreið,Laugavegi 16, tel: 511 6060, www.eyjar.is. Very nice tourist hotel right in the centre of Reykjavik. $$

Lykil Hotel, Borgartun 32, tel: 511 6030, www.keyhotels.is. New tourist hotel, small rooms but can be a good deal. About 25 minutes walk into the centre. $$

Baldursbrá, Laufásvegur 41, IS-101 Reykjavík, tel: 552 6646, tel: 562 6647; www. artemis.centrum.is/~heijfis. Eight double rooms and a few spaces for sleeping bags. Regular guests return each year. $.

Reykjavík Youth Hostel, Sundlaugavegur 34, IS-105 Reykjavík, tel: 553 8110, fax: 588 9201, www.hostel.is. Functional hostel with about 100 beds. Often noisy in the morning as guests leave early. Good position near swimming pool, but 30 minutes' walk from the centre. $.

Room With a View Apartments, Laugarvegar 18, IS-101 Reykjavík, tel: 5527262, email: arnike@mm.is, www.roomwithaview.is. Penthouse apartments on the main street in the centre of Reykjavík. Great view over the city; some apartments have access to a jacuzzi on the balcony. Can accommodate 1–7 persons.

Salvation Army Guesthouse, Kirkjustræti 2, tel: 561 3203, fax: 561 3315. This is the most inexpensive guesthouse in Reykjavík. No-frills facilities, but neat and clean. The location is excellent – right in the town centre. There are facilities for cooking on the ground floor. $

Hótel Edda

Akureyri
Fosshótel KEA, Hafnarstræti 89, tel: 460 2000, fax: 460 2060. The town's traditional hotel offering international standards and a restaurant. $$$.
Hótel Norðurland (Key Hótel), Geislagötu 7, tel: 462 2600, fax: 462 7962. Comfortable, but rather ordinary hotel near to the town hall square. $$$.
Fosshótel Björk, Hafnarstræti 67, tel: 461 3030, fax: 461 3033. Informal 19-room hotel near the town centre, with a view of the fjord. $$$.
Hótel Edda, Eyarlandsvegur 28, tel: 461 1434, fax: 461 1423. Older summer hotel near the swimming pool. $–$$.
v/Þórunnarstræti campsite, tel: 462 3379. Centrally-located near the swimming pool. Lively, sometimes loud.

Arnastapi
Ferðaþjónustan Snjófell, IS-355 Arnastapi, tel: 435 6783, fax: 453 6795. Accommodation (with space for sleeping bags), restaurant, tourist information and excursions. $.

Ásbyrgi
Tjaldsvæfi Ásbyrgi, IS-641 Húsavík, tel: 465 2195. The National Park runs two campsites here. The one at the entrance is very well equipped, the other rather basic.

Borgarnes
Hótel Borgarnes, Egilsgata 14-16, IS-310 Borgarnes, tel: 437 1119, fax: 437 1443. Pleasant, upmarket hotel with good restaurant. $$.
Hyrnan campsite near the petrol station on the edge of town. Brúartorg, IS-310 Borgarnes, tel: 437 2108, fax: 437 1960. Modern service area, with wide range of 24-hour facilities including cafeteria. $.

Breiðavík
Breiðavík, Látrabjarg, IS-451 Patreksfjörður, tel: 456 1575, fax: 456 1189. Basic but well-run summer accommodation in an old boarding school; space for sleeping bags; small cafeteria. $.

Breiddalsvík
Hótel Bláfell, IS-760 Breiddalsvík, tel: 475 6770, fax: 475 6668. Rooms are of varying standard; space for sleeping bags. The restaurant has received international awards. $$.
Berunes Youth Hostel, tel: 478 8988. Pleasant hostel in an old farmhouse.

The harbour at Djúpivogur

Djúpivogur
Hótel Framtið, Vogarland 4, IS-765 Djúpivogur, tel: 478 8887, fax: 478 8187. Friendly hotel in an old Danish trading centre; space for sleeping bags; fish restaurant. $$.

Egilsstaðir and environs
Hótel Hérað (Icelandair Hótel), tel: 471 1500, fax: 471 1501. Modern (1998), upmarket hotel open all year. $$$.
Edda Hótel, tel: 471 2775, fax: 505 0522. The house next door offers basic rooms in the summer months. $–$$.
Campsite, tel: 471 2001. Noisy campsite near the shopping centre and service area. Waste-disposal facilities.
Gistiheimilið Eiðum, IS-705 Eiðar, tel/fax: 471 3846. Basic summer hostel in Eiðar's primary school 12km (7 miles) north of Egilsstaðir, with the choice of double or family rooms. $.
Hótel Edda Eiðar, tel: 505 0522, fax: 471 3870. Boarding school summer hotel; indoor pool and restaurant. $.
Hússtjórnarskólinn, IS-707 Hallormsstaður, tel: 471 1761. Summer hotel, 12 basic rooms in old college. $.
Fosshótel Hallormstaður, tel: 471 1705, fax: 562 5895. Woodland summer hotel by the Lögurinn lake. $–$$.
Atlavík campsite, Hallormstaður. Idyllic lakeside spot in the woods.
Skipalækur (west of the Largarfljót bridge), tel: 471 1324. Tourist-style farmhouse accommodation with almost 80 beds in various buildings and cabins; horses for hire, snow scooters in winter. Fishing permits for sale. $.
Farfuglaheimilið Húsey, Tunguhreppur, IS-701 Egilsstaðir, tel: 471 3010, fax: 471 3009. Nearest shops in Egilsstaðir. $.

Flatey
Veitingastofan Vogur, tel: 438 1413. Basic summer accommodation with space for sleeping bags; cafeteria. $.

Goðafoss
Gistihúsið Fosshóll, v/Goðafoss, IS-645 Fosshóll, tel: 464 3108, fax: 464 3318. Farmhouse accommodation close to the Goðafoss. Made-up beds, hostel with space for sleeping bags, well-equipped campsite and all-day cafeteria ($). Locally-run co-operative sells handicrafts.

Grindavík
Hótel Bláa Lónið, tel: 426 8650, fax: 426 8651. Affordable, family-run hotel close to the Blue Lagoon. Transfers can be arranged to and from Keflavík airport. $$.

Hellissandur
Gistihúsið Gimli, Keflavíkurgata 4, IS-360 Hellissandur, tel: 436 6825, fax: 436 6770. Hostel-style pension with space for sleeping bags; kitchen for self-caterers. $.

Höfn
Stafafell í Lón, IS-781 Höfn, tel: 478 1717, fax: 478 1785. Farmstead with youth hostel, farmhouse accommodation,

Goðafoss accommodation and falls

space for sleeping bags and campsite. Jeep tours to the hiking areas in the hinterland. $–$$.

Hótel Höfn (Icelandair Hótel), tel: 478 1240, fax: 478 1996. Central hotel with all modern conveniences. $$$.

Ásgarður, guesthouse under the same management (space for sleeping bags). $$.

Hótel Edda Nesjaskóli, tel: 478 1470, fax: 505 0522. Typical summer hotel with space for sleeping bags, about 7km (4 miles) outside the town near the airport; coaches and scheduled buses from and to the west stop here. $–$$.

Gistiheimilið Hvammur, Ránarslóð, tel: 478 1503, fax: 478 1591. Eight-room pension by the harbour. $.

Well-equipped campsite on the outskirts of town by the Travel Centre. Tel: 478 1701, fax: 478 1901.

Húsafell

Húsafell Service Center, tel: 435 1377, fax: 435 1463. Well-equipped campsite and basic hostel ($) next to a geothermally heated swimming pool.

Húsavík

Húsavík

Hótel Húsavík, Ketilsbraut 22, IS-640 Húsavík, tel: 464 1220, fax: 464 2161. Modern and functional. $$$.

Árból, Ásgarðsvegur 2, tel: 464 2220, fax: 464 1463. Pleasant bed and breakfast, close to the town centre. $.

Hveragerði

Hótel Örk (Key Hótel), Breiðamörk 1, tel: 483 4700, fax: 483 4755. Luxury hotel on the outskirts of the town. Excellent restaurant and thermal baths. $$$.

Hveravellir landscape

Hveravellir

Ferðafélag mountain cabins by Hvítárvatn and in Hveravellir. Also campsites.

Hvolsvöllur

Hótel Hvolsvöllur, Hlíðarvegur 7, IS-860 Hvolsvöllur, tel: 487 8187, fax: 487 8391. Convenient hotel with restaurant, open all year round. $–$$.

Ísafjörður

Hótel Ísafjörður, Silfurtorg, tel: 456 4111, fax: 456 4767. Central, modern hotel building; good restaurant. $$$.

Framhaldsskólinn campsite, tel: 456 4485. Space for sleeping bags in an edge-of-town boarding school. $–$$.

Kirkjubæjarklaustur

Hótel Kirkjubæjarklaustur (Icelandair Hótel), tel: 487 4799, fax: 487 4614. A functional summer hotel ($–$$, space for sleeping bags) and a very comfortable hotel wing ($$$), open all year; swimming pool and restaurant.

Laugarvatn

Hótel Edda Íkí Laugarvatn, tel: 486 1154, fax: 505 0522. The more comfortable of the two Edda hotels in the town; restaurant. $$.

Lýsuhóll

Lýsuhóll farmhouse, Staðarsveit, IS-355 Ólafsvík, tel: 435 6716, fax: 435 6816. Space for sleeping bags; whirlpool with spring water for guests. $.

Mývatn

Hótel Reynihlíð, tel: 464 4170, fax: 464 4371. Lake Myvatn's top hotel; popular restaurant, which can get busy with coach tours. $$$.

Hótel Ísafjörður

Hótel Reykjahlíð, tel: 464 4142, fax: 464 4336. Fully renovated, with 13 rooms. Enjoys a magnificent lakeside position. $$.

Farm Stöng, tel: 464 4252, fax: 464 4352. A farmhouse about 10km (7 miles) from the southwestern tip of the lake. Space for 50 guests, meals available. $.

Farm Stöng

Skútustaðaskóli, tel: 464 4279. Basic summer accommodation in a school; plenty of space for sleeping bags. $.

Bjarg/Eldá Travel Services, tel: 464 4220, fax: 464 4321. Private bed and breakfast ($) and a popular campsite. Open 15 May–30 September. Situated by the lake and used by many independent travellers, Eldá organises round trips and sells tickets for tourist amenities provided by other companies.

Tjaldsvæði Reykjahlíð, tel: 464 4103, fax: 464 4305. Well-equipped campsite, popular with groups. Space for sleeping bags in huts. Open 1 June–10 September.

Nýidalur

Ferðafélag mountain cabins by the main route and by Laugarfell (with hot pool) by the F752, 30km/19 miles to the northwest towards Varmahlip.

Ólafsvík

Höfdi, Ólafsbraut 20, IS-355 Ólafsvík, tel: 436 1650, fax: 463 1651. A 14-room guest house with restaurant on the main street; can arrange glacier tours. $.

Þingvellir

Hótel Valhöll (Key Hótel), tel: 482 2622, fax: 482 3622. Traditional hotel below Almannagjá rift by lakeside. Open summer only. Good restaurant serving fresh trout. $$–$$$. Several campsites in the National Park.

Reykholt

Hótel Reykholt, IS-320 Reykholt, tel: 435 1260, fax: 435 1421. Summer hotel in a modern boarding school. $.

Reykir
Sæberg, Reykir, IS-500 Brú, tel: 451 0015, fax: 451 0034. Friendly and inexpensive hostel. $.

Staðarskáli
Staðarskáli, IS-500 Staðarhreppur, tel: 451 1150, fax: 451 1107. Away from service area. Some basic rooms, plus pleasant country-style restaurant. $–$$.

Sauðárkrókur
Fosshótel Áning, v/Sæmundarhlíp, 550 Sauðárkrókur, tel: 453 6717, fax: 453 6087. Modern, well-equipped summer hotel with excellent restaurant. $$.

Reykjadalur
Narfastaðir, tel: 464 3102, fax: 464 3319. Farmhouse accommodation with over 50 beds. $–$$.
Fosshótel Laugar, tel: 464 3340, fax: 464 3163. Summer hotel in a boarding school; thermal baths; restaurant. $.

Reykjanes
Ferðaþjónustan Reykjanes, IS-401 Ísafjörður, tel: 456 4844, fax: 456 4845. Spacious complex with rooms, space for sleeping bags and camping area; many facilities for the active. $.
Hótel Djúpavík, tel: 451 4037. Basic hotel in an old hostel for workers at the fish factory. $.

Strokkur geysir

Selfoss
Hótel Selfoss, Eyrarvegur 2, IS-800 Selfoss, tel: 482 2500, fax: 482 2524. Modern business hotel in town centre; restaurant. $$$. About 100 metres away, the more basic **Hótel Þóristún**, is under the same management. $$.
Hótel Geysir, IS-801 Selfoss, tel: 486 8915, fax: 486 8715. Hotel with space for sleeping bags. $.

Seyðisfjörður
Hótel Snæfell, Austurvegur 3, tel: 472 1460, fax: 472 1570. Timber house in centre of town. Friendly ambience. Only nine rooms. Restaurant ($$$) serves good fish. $–$$.
Farfuglaheimilið Hafaldan, Ránargata 9, tel: 472 1410, fax: 472 1486. Rather primitive hostel. Dormitories. $.

Fun in the snow

Skaftafell National Park
Hótel Skaftafell, Freysnes, IS-785 Fagurhólsmyri, tel: 478 1945, fax: 478 1846. Functional but pleasant hotel with space for sleeping bags in an annexe. Just under 4km (2½ miles) east of the National Park; restaurant. $$.
Hof í Öræfum, IS-755 Fagurhólsmýri, tel: 478 1669, fax: 478 1638. Farmhouse 20km (12 miles) from Skaftafell National Park. Also sleeping-bag accommodation. $–$$.

Well-equipped campsite near the service and information centre. Tel: 478 1627.

Skógar
Hótel Edda Skógar, tel: 487 8870, fax: 505 0522. In an old school building between the museum and waterfall. $.

Stykkishólmur
Hótel Stykkishólmur, Vatnsás, IS-340, tel: 438 1330, fax: 438 1579. Sombre appearance, but a great view; restaurant. $$$.
Hótel Eyjaferðir, Aðalgata 8, tel: 438 1450, fax: 438 1050. Central position. Book via the Eyjaferðir travel agency. $$.

Varmaland
Varmaland Guesthouse, tel: 435 1303, fax: 435 1307. Hostel-style accommodation near the Ring Road. $.

Varmahlíð
Hótel Varmahlíð, IS-560 Varmahlíð, tel: 453 8170, fax: 453 8870. Small hotel with restaurant, open all year. $$.

Vík í Mýrdal
Hótel Vík, Klettsvegur, tel: 487 1480, fax: 487 1302. New hotel near the service area; arranges summer home lets. $$. Large campsite opposite Víkurskáli service area. Tel: 487 1345 or Vík tourist information office.
Guesthouse Reynisbrekka, Myrdal, 870, tel: 487 1106; fax: 487 1303. Just outside Vík, this is a basic hostel. $

Vatnajökull
Jöklasel, tel: 478 1001 or Höfn tourist information office *(see page 91)*. Mountain cabin with space for 30 sleeping bags (only groups in winter).

Hótel Edda Skógar

Trekking among the Westfjords

Index

Accommodation...........95
Aldeyjarfoss................69
Álftafjörður................44
Akureyri.................32–3
Almannagjá gorge......66
Almannaskarð pass.....45
Arnarfjörður................60
Arnastapi....................55
art.............................74
Ásbyrgi gorge..............39
Askja caldera..............71
Austurhorn.................44

Berserkjahraun
lava field................57
Berufjörður................44
Bláa Lonið..................25
Bogarvirki fortress......30
Borgarnes...................53
Breiðafjörður..............58
Breiðárlón glacial lake 46
Breiðavík....................59
Breiddalsvík.............43–4
Búðir......................54–5

Cape Bjargtangar........59
cinema.......................74
climate....................7–8
cuisine.......................77

Dalatangi....................43
Dettifoss.................38, 39
Dimmuborgir..............36
Djúpavík.....................62
Djúpivogur.................44
Drangey island............31
Drekagil gorge............71
Dritvík.......................55
Dynjandi waterfall......60
Dyrhólaey..................49

Economy.................10–11
Egilsstaðir..................40
Eiríksjökull.................29
Eldborg volcano.........54

Fagurhólsmýri............46
festivals.....................75
Fjarðará canyon..........48
Flatey island...............58
flora and fauna............9

Geography...................6
geology....................5–6
Glaumbær
Folk Museum...........30
Goðafoss.............34, 69
Grábrók crater............29

Grenjaðarstaður Folk
Museum..................38
Grímsey island............34
Grímsstaðir................38
Grjótagjá caves...........37
Gullfoss................65, 68

Hafnarfjörður..............25
Hallormsstaður...........40
Hamarsfjörður............44
Hamarsrétt.................30
Heimaey island.......50–1
Hekla volcano............64
Hellisgerði lava park...25
Hellissandur...............56
Hellnar......................55
Hengifoss...................41
Herðubreið volcano..70–1
Hindisvík seal bay.......30
history...................14–15
Hjálparfoss.................64
Hjörleifshöfði.............48
Höfði woodland park..36
Höfn...........................45
Hofsós.......................31
Hólar..........................31
Hólmavík...................62
Hóp tidal lake.............30
Hrafnseyri vicarage.....60
Hraunfossar................29
Húsafell.....................29
Húsavík...................38–9
Hvalfjörður.................28
Hvannadalshnúkur......46
Hveragerði.................50
Hverarönd geothermal
field......................37
Hverfell.....................36
Hveravellir.................68
Hvítárvatn glacial lake.68
Hvítserkur..................30
Hvolsvöllur................50

Ingólfshöfði island.....46
Ísafjörður...................61

Jökulsárgljúfur
National Park...........39
Jökulsárlón glacial lake46
Jökulsá á Brú river.....40

Katla volcano..............48
Kerið crater................63
Kirkjubæjarklaustur....47
Kirkjufell...................57
Kjölur plateau............68
Krafla.........................38
Kverkfjöll massif.........71

Lake Mývatn...........35–7
Laki crater.................48
Landmannalaugar.......49
Langjökull..............29, 68
language....................10
Látrabjarg cliffs..........59
Laufás local history
museum..................34
Laugavatn..................65
lava caves..................29
literature................73–4
Litlanesfoss................41
Lögurinn.....................40
Lómagnúpur...............47
Lóndrangar.................55
Lúdent.......................36
Lundey island.............39

Maritime Museum.......25
Midnight sun...............8
Minjasafn Egils
Ólafssonar museum..58
Mjóifjörður.................43
Möðrudalur..........39, 71
Morsárjökull...............46
Mount Helgafell.........57
music.........................74
Mýrdalssandur...........48

Námaskarð.................37
nightlife.....................80
Núpsstaður farmstead..47
Nýja-Eldhraun
lava field.............47–8

Ólafsvík.....................57
Öxarfjörður inlet........39

Papey island...............44
people..............7, 9–10
Þingeyri....................60
Þingvallavatn.............66
Þingvellir...................66
Þjóðveldisbærinn
Viking house........64–5
Þjórsárdalur.............64–5
politics..................12–13
Þórisvatn...................69
Þórsmörk Valley.........49
Prestagil ravine..........43
Prestbakki church.......62
Pyrill mountain..........28

Religion.....................10
restaurants.............78–9
Reykholt....................29
Reykir........................30
Reykjafjörður.............60

Reykjahlíð..............36–7
Reykjanes peninsula....62
Reykjavík..............18–25

Sagas.........................13
Sænautasel farmhouse 40
Sauðárkrókur.............31
Selfoss..................39, 50
Seljahjallagil gorge.....36
Seljalandsfoss.............49
Seljavellir...................49
Seyðisfjörður..............41
Sigulfjörður................31
Skaftafell
National Park...........46
Skálafellsjökull...........45
Skálholt.....................64
Skeidarársandur.........47
Skógafoss...................49
Skriduklaustur............40
Skrúður bird rock........43
Skútustaðagígar
pseudo-crater..........36
Snæfell......................41
Snæfellsjökull..........54–5
Snæfellsnes peninsula .54
Sólheimajökull...........49
sports........................81
Sprengisandur............69
Staðarskáli.............29–30
Steingrímsfjarðarheiði
plateau...................62
Stöðvarfjörður............43
Stóragjá caves............37
Stóri-Geysir...............65
Strandir coast............62
Strokkur geyser..........65
Suðurnes (Reykjanes) .25
Stykkishólmur..........57–8
Súgandisey island.....57–8
Svartifoss...................46

Tourist information..90–1
transport.................83–9

Valþjófsstaður church..40
Varmahlíð...................30
Varmaland..................29
Vatnajökull.....41, 45–6
Vattarnes lighthouse...43
Viðimyri church..........30
Vigur island................61
Vík í Mýrdal............48–9
Víti crater..................71

Westman Islands......50–1
whale-watching12, 38, 57
whaling..................11–12